BEFORE FIRST GRADE

Early Childhood Education Series
Kenneth D. Wann, Editor

BEFORE FIRST GRADE
Susan W. Gray, Rupert A. Klaus, James O. Miller, and
Bettye J. Forrester

NEW DIRECTIONS IN THE KINDERGARTEN
Helen F. Robison and Bernard Spodek

THE YOUNG DISADVANTAGED
Margaret Yonemura, Rose Mukerji, and Ruth Hamlin

PARENTS AND CHILDREN LEARN TOGETHER:
Parent Cooperative Nursery Schools
Katharine Whiteside Taylor

CHILDREN DISCOVER MUSIC AND DANCE
Emma D. Sheehy

BEFORE
FIRST
GRADE

THE EARLY TRAINING PROJECT FOR CULTURALLY DISADVANTAGED CHILDREN

Susan W. Gray
Rupert A. Klaus
James O. Miller
Bettye J. Forrester

TEACHERS COLLEGE PRESS
Teachers College, Columbia University
New York, 1966

© 1966 by Teachers College, Columbia University
Library of Congress Catalog Card Number: 66-24872
Manufactured in the United States of America
Third Printing, 1969

Cover design by Moneta Barnett

CONTENTS

FOREWORD

The current development of programs to prevent educational retardation sharply focuses the need for activities designed to compensate for the deprivation that some children experience in their homes and communities. These youngsters require curriculums that are specifically shaped to build their motivation for learning and to provide activities and direct teaching for concept and language development. There is an urgent need in the rapidly multiplying programs for culturally disadvantaged children for help in defining and implementing activities that will directly meet their developmental requirements.

The authors of *Before First Grade* recognize this problem. They have brought together a handbook of techniques and materials that have emerged from several years of working with groups of young disadvantaged children. Readers may recognize many of the approaches and materials customarily found in nursery schools and kindergartens. The essential difference, however, lies in the authors' conscious attempt to identify specific needs of the children and to develop lesson plans and teaching procedures to meet them. The book delineates day-by-day activities in a way that makes it possible to see the relationship between the procedures employed and the aims they were designed to accomplish.

The authors believe that the *how* of their activities is of much greater significance than the *what:* the way that materials are used is more important, generally speaking, than are the particular materials in themselves. Here is a program emphasizing the adaptation of equipment and methods to the unique pattern of abilities and interests of each child. The authors believe that this individualization, while important to all children, is of particular significance to deprived children, since one aspect of their problem seems to be that they lack a sense of individual worth as a result of the failure of the adults in their world to appreciate each child's individual pattern of competencies and concerns.

This handbook will be of great value to supervisors, teachers, aides, and volunteer workers who are developing educational programs for young disadvantaged children. In addition to suggesting specific activities, it presents a conceptual scheme for preschool intervention which can be easily adapted to other situations and to children of various ages.

KENNETH D. WANN

Teachers College, Columbia University
July, 1966

* * *

The authors wish to acknowledge the help of many persons in the inception and bringing to completion of this handbook. Especial thanks are due Alma Davis, one of two head teachers, who prepared much of the material for Chapter IV, and Della Horton, home visitor, who wrote most of the material in Chapter VI. We should also like to express appreciation to our other head teacher, Mary Craighead, and to Doris Outlaw, who also served as home visitor. We are grateful for the support, encouragement, and help provided by Baxter Hobgood, Superintendent of the Murfreesboro (Tennessee) schools, and by Emma Roberts, Principal of Bradley School in Murfreesboro. Most of all, we wish to express our thanks to the children and the mothers with whom we have worked during the past four years. The cooperation of the parents has been the essential element in our ability to carry on our study. The children have been a continual source of delight to us.

The Early Training Project is supported by the National Institute of Mental Health, under Mental Health Project Grant 5-R11-MH00765. Additional support for research staff has been made possible by Grant HD-00973 from the National Institute of Child Health and Human Development, from the United States Office of Education, Contract OE-6-10-193 and Grant 66-9174 from the Office of Economic Opportunity.

SUSAN W. GRAY, RUPERT A. KLAUS,
JAMES O. MILLER, BETTYE J. FORRESTER

George Peabody College for Teachers
Nashville, Tennessee

I

THE EARLY TRAINING PROJECT: AN OVERVIEW

The Early Training Project is a research-demonstration study which has as its primary concern the planning and carrying through of a particular intervention program for young deprived children. The major question behind the project is whether it is possible, following a carefully designed program of intervention prior to school entrance, to offset the progressive retardation all too frequently observed in deprived children during their years of schooling. Typically, such children enter first grade a little behind more favored children, and, as the years go by, the gap widens, so that by the end of elementary school the deprived child will have fallen two or three years behind the others.

The children with whom we have worked live in a town of about 25,000 in the upper south; the sample is Negro. The population of the town is highly stable; during the three years of our study, for example, we lost only two of eighty-seven families. Most of the families are at least third generation in the vicinity and came originally from a predominantly agricultural background. Until quite recently opportunities for upward mobility of Negroes remaining in this city have been slight. Employment of mothers in our sample is chiefly as domestics, as kitchen help in restaurants, or as maids in beauty parlors. In the homes with fathers, workers tend to be unskilled or semi-skilled—truck drivers, porters, building custodians—a few are employed in skilled trades in construction work. Families are large, the median number of children being five; about forty per cent have no fathers in the home. In most of the families responsibility for child care is shared by grandmothers, aunts, and older sisters. Our criteria for selection of families were the following: housing conditions (including furnishings and educational and cultural materials present), occupation, education of parents, and income.

From all Negro children born in the city in 1958, we selected sixty as coming from the most deprived families according to the criteria we used. These children were then randomized into three treatment groups. The first group went through a training sequence that consisted of three special summer school experiences of ten weeks each plus contacts with a specially trained home visitor in the months between the summer experiences. The second group went through a similar sequence which began a year later, however; they have had two summer experiences, and one winter of home visitor contacts. The third group is the control group which receives all the pretests and post-tests, but has had no experimental treatment other than a weekly play session instituted during the last summer for purposes of public relations. There is, in addition, a fourth control group of twenty-seven in a similar city sixty miles distant. Since the first community is small, and the families live in a fairly restricted geographical area, we thought that communication between families would be great. Thus, we expected that the work we would be doing with the children would be a common topic of discussion with the result that parents of the control group would attempt to duplicate as much as possible our efforts with the experimental children. Such response on the part of the non-experimental parents would create a diffusion of treatment effect. To assess this diffusion effect, a distal group was deemed necessary. The children in all of these groups entered first grade in September of 1964. A home visitor continued to visit in the home of the two experimental groups during the first grade. The table on the facing page indicates the general design of the study.

Each group of approximately twenty children had a head teacher selected as a master primary teacher. During the first two summers there was a teaching assistant for every five children; during the last summer, one for every six or seven children. The high adult-child ratio and the attention given to daily and weekly lesson plans made possible an individualized and specific program. The staff was balanced about equally as to race and sex. We

LAYOUT OF GENERAL RESEARCH DESIGN

Treatments	T_1-three summer schools	T_2-two summer schools	T_3-local controls	T_4-distal controls
First winter 1961-1962	(Criterion and curriculum development)			
First summer 1962	pretest summer school post-test	pretest post-test	pretest post-test	pretest post-test
Second winter 1962-1963	home visitor contacts			
Second summer 1963	pretest summer school post-test	pretest summer school post-test	pretest post-test	pretest post-test
Third winter 1963-1964	home visitor contacts	home visitor contacts		
Third summer 1964	pretest summer school post-test	pretest summer school post-test	pretest post-test	pretest post-test
Fourth winter 1964-1965	home visitor contacts follow-up tests	home visitor contacts follow-up tests	follow-up tests	follow-up tests
Fifth winter 1965-1966	follow-up tests	follow-up tests	follow-up tests	follow-up tests

believed it particularly important to have men teachers to serve as father-figures and as achieving role models for the boys, many of whom were without fathers in the home. We felt the integrated staff particularly desirable with these children who heretofore had had little experience with white persons.

The summer experiences focused attention on two main classes of variables:

(a) attitudes toward achievement—including achievement motivation, persistence, delay of gratification, interest in school-type activities, and identification with achieving role models.

(b) aptitudes for achievement—including percept development, concept formation, and language development.

The home visitor contacts over the rest of the year focused on providing continuity with the summer preschool through providing materials as well as through reinforcing and supporting both child and parents in terms of the experimental variables. In addition, the home visitor emphasized the value of making the mother more aware of the possible opportunities for Negroes in the present and in the future, and of enabling her to develop a more realistic picture of the instrumental steps involved in preparing a child to take advantage of such opportunities.

We have collected a great deal of data on the children and a certain amount on the parents. Our crucial comparisons, however, must wait until the future, since our major concern is with school progress. It is only now that the children are well into school that we can see whether the particular experimental package we have put together is as efficacious as we would hope. Not until the children have been in school for two or three years will we be able to see whether any such effects have a degree of permanence.

At the time of school entrance our first experimental group showed a gain of nine IQ points, a modest change, but one maintained over two and one-half years. The second experimental group showed a gain of five points, while the local control group had lost three points, and the distal group, six points. Similar findings were obtained for measures of language and certain aspects of concept development. What seems to be occurring is a diffusion effect in the local control group, for these children have made considerable gains during their year in school. The distal control group has not shown as much gain. Further analyses and studies of the children during the next few years will be necessary before we can assess more adequately the long-range results of this kind of intervention program. A diffusion effect to other ıildren and families with whom the experimental children and ıothers are associated would be the most hopeful result we could ınd. We need additional data, however, before we can be sure ıat this is indeed a diffusion effect and not a result attributable ı other aspects of the life situations of the children in the first ıree treatment groups.

II

ATTITUDE DEVELOPMENT

One of the overarching purposes of the Early Training Projec was to develop in the children attitudes that would be conduciv to active participation in the learning process of the school, pai ticularly with respect to motivation to achieve and to such relate variables as persistence and the ability to delay gratification. W were also concerned with developing interest in school-type activ ties and in promoting the child's identification with achieving ro models. Our general procedure in bringing this about was base upon a carefully planned approach to reinforcing that behavior i children which we believed, on the basis of research, would b most conducive to adequate school performance. The followin chapter describes in some detail our reinforcement procedures an the particular ways in which we attempted to promote those att tudes which appear to us to be crucial to success in school.

REINFORCEMENT PROCEDURES

Reinforcement is a technical term used to signify the cons quences, in terms of reward and punishment, for the behavic or responses of individuals. Generally speaking, the reinforceme which an individual receives for a performance will be critical i determining whether or not that performance will be repeate Another way of expressing it is to say that results are major dete minants of what the individual learns. Positive reinforceme (reward) is usually more effective than negative reinforceme (punishment), particularly when one is concerned with learnir

6

ᴉew responses. It also has more desirable effects from the stand-
ᴉoint of the personal development of a child. In the Early Train-
ᴉg Project we were concerned almost entirely with positive rein-
ᴉrcement. Our major problems were to select what behavior
ᴉhould be reinforced and to decide what kind of positive reinforce-
ᴉent should be used. We started by looking at the probable char-
ᴉcteristic patterns of reinforcement in the homes from which the
ᴉhildren in our project came.

To summarize these patterns, we find the situation for the
ᴉeprived child, when compared to more favored middle class
ᴉhildren, to be somewhat as follows:

1. The culturally deprived child generally receives less rein-
ᴉrcement of his behavior.

2. The reinforcement of the culturally deprived child is some-
ᴉhat less adult-administered than that of the middle class child.
ᴉhis happens because the mother is apt to be home less, there-
ᴉre she is less often available for reinforcement. The mother's
ᴉhysical and emotional energies are so drained into maintaining
ᴉ subsistence level in the home that she has little energy left over
ᴉr patterning her child's behavior. All she can do is to try to
ᴉope with the behavior of the minute.

3. The reinforcement the culturally deprived child receives
ᴉ not likely to be verbal. The more probable forms of reinforce-
ᴉent he receives are tangible and physical, coming directly from
ᴉhe situation. It is a form of self-reinforcement which restricts his
ᴉnctioning to a primitive, concrete level. His concept of important
ᴉbjects and behavior remains tied to their use or utility—that is,
ᴉr him, a horse is to ride, a wagon is to pull, and an apple is to
ᴉat. He probably receives a fair amount of nonverbal social rein-
ᴉrcement (pats, hugs, shoves, and the like) from his peers and
ᴉiblings.

4. The reinforcement of the culturally deprived child is less
ᴉocused in terms of being directed toward the adequacy or inade-
ᴉuacy of his specific acts. In other words, his reinforcement is
ᴉpt to consist of a rather vague, generalized approval such as,
ᴉThat's a good boy," or merely a smile, rather than such specific
ᴉpproving words as, "You tied your shoes just right," or, "You
ᴉeally did a good job of helping me with the sweeping." The

vague approval does not help the child develop his own standard
of performance.

5. Reinforcement is directed more towards inhibiting behavior
than it is toward encouraging exploratory activities. Again, this
is the picture of the mother's need to cope with the behavior
rather than to shape it. In other words, she is more concerned
with a child's not being troublesome than she is with his learning
more about his world.

6. Reinforcement, when it comes for the culturally deprived
child, is likely to be immediate; there is little stress on the child
learning to delay gratification. This is such an important element
of the total picture of development that it will be a subject of
another section, and is only mentioned here.

These characteristics of the life situation of the culturally
deprived child have certain implications as to how one may use
positive reinforcement effectively with such youngsters. First, they
suggest that when one starts to work with youngsters from such
homes he will find that the best approaches are nonverbal social
reinforcement—patting, hugging, carrying around, letting the child
sit in his lap—and concrete reward—such as small pieces of
candy, cookies, lollipops, balloons, and little plastic toys. One will
also find that the reward needs to be immediate, as soon as possible after the desired response has been made.

This is how one starts, but over the years prior to school
entrance one needs to move toward the following:

(a) more verbal rewards, for example, less hugging and more
praising. One also needs to move toward rewards that are less
concrete; tokens, gold stars, and the like, may eventually be used
as symbols of adult approval of the child's acts.

(b) more delayed rewards.

(c) greater reward value of "bookish" objects and activities
such as books, crayons, drawing paper, and records.

(d) more *specific* reinforcement in terms of the child's performance. That is, in reinforcing behavior, one should help the
child focus on the aspects of his performance that are correct or
incorrect.

(e) as time goes on one needs to become increasingly
selective in reinforcement. At the beginning of preschool, the

teacher's task is primarily one of using whatever methods he can to get the child to interact with his environment. Later, one should move toward selective reinforcement of such things as exploratory behavior designed to find out about new things or to discover new relationships, conspicuous efforts to achieve, to persist towards a goal, to put off immediate gratification for that more delayed, and attempts to correct inadequate performances, such as wanting to do over a drawing that the child did not feel was quite right. In other words, one tries to be aware of the growing edge of the child's behavior, so that one is reinforcing him not for the things which are easy for him to do but for those things that are just within his level of ability.

In general, one should keep in mind that an interested, reinforcing adult has tremendous impact on young children, particularly deprived children who have received inadequate rewards from adults. This means that teachers and other workers with young children will have tremendous power in shaping the child's efforts and activities. One can couple one's social approval of a nonverbal, physical sort with verbal social approval, and also later with more abstract and delayed rewards. As an example, one may find as the months go by that the child will recognize that such token rewards as gold stars, little trinkets, or colored seals stand for a measure of the adult's approval of his activities.

The next step from such abstract and symbolic rewards is the child's internalizing of his own reward systems, building up his own standards of performance. One can hardly hope to have preschool children do very much internalizing; it can be helped, however, by encouraging the child to set his own standards, to evaluate his own performance, or by such simple techniques as trying to arouse the child's pride in his activities—"Aren't you proud that you painted such a good picture!"

ACHIEVEMENT MOTIVATION

McClelland defines achievement motivation as competition with an internalized standard of excellence. We would also include in this definition effort extended over a long period of time as well as the ability to postpone immediate gratification for long-term goals. These latter abilities, however, are being considered separately as persistence and delay of gratification. In other words, here we have broken down achievement motivation into several components and are discussing them separately, although we would agree with McClelland that they are part of the total concept. Other important aspects of achievement motivation are striving to learn something new, to improve one's previous performance, and to do for oneself rather than being done for.

Research findings indicate that achievement motivation is associated more with middle class than lower class children. They also suggest that achievement motivation is associated with early home training in independence and with considerable reinforcement from the mother, especially in terms of affection. Presumably it could be concluded from these studies that an effective approach would be to use liberal reinforcement, particularly the conveying of affection and approval of the child's efforts to be independent, to do it himself, to better his previous record, and of the attempt to meet adult standards of performance which are just a trifle beyond the child's present level of performance.

In applying the results of these studies, however, we must observe a delicate distinction. Being culturally deprived, some children will be far from being able to internalize such striving toward excellence. The most accessible path and probably the most effective one to follow in leading them to internalize and to move away from more concrete rewards is to show affection and approval of each child's efforts to achieve. Some of these children appear starved for affection and blossom like flowers from the warmth of a friendly hug. Here lies the dilemma, however, the tenuous balance between nurturing affective bonds and using affection as reinforcement for internalizing standards of excellence. To be sure, close relationships between adult training staff and the children will develop but it must always be remembered that the training period has time limits and the necessity of severing relationships built over the training period must be considered. This is a sort of weaning process whereby efforts are made to help the children internalize and, perhaps to a lesser extent, to transfer to their next year's teacher such reward value for work well done. Thus, the use of affection has its pitfalls as well as its most important contribution of reinforcement for internalization of achievement motives.

In making the transition from specific affective bonds to achievement-oriented values, some sort of concrete evidence of the child's training experience for him to keep is particularly important. It is often noticed in play therapy that for some children it is very meaningful for them to have tangible evidence of their play therapy contacts when the series of interviews is over. Some possible methods of approach are given in the following paragraphs.

1. It must be emphasized that the training program is a process and that one must be alert to process changes. Unless the developmental aspects of the program are constantly kept in mind, instructional efforts can become routinized in a way that can very well lead to fixation in method and procedures. From what has already been said, it should also be noted that there are limits to the training period. It requires thoughtfulness and effective planning to prepare the child to accept these limits but to continue operating in his daily life with what he has learned and experienced. Discussing at home activities which have an achievement motif provides a transition from experiences in the training program to the child's daily life at home. Games are particularly effective activities for encouraging the children to work at bettering their performance away from the school site. "Did you bounce the ball more times last night at home, Joe, than you did at school?" the teacher might ask.

With children of this age, relationship with a mother-figure, and to a lesser extent with a father-figure, is paramount in their functioning. In terms of bringing them closer to regular school, the view that the lead teacher is their teacher and the rest of those assisting are helpers must be kept before them as clearly as possible. It must be remembered that the personal relationship is probably the most effective way of motivating the children, but also the one from which they must be weaned, although not too severely or abruptly, when the training is over. It is necessary to do a good bit of preparing of the children for the close of the training period, for instance, by discussing it with them together and individually and by giving them a week or longer to adjust to the idea.

2. The question of reinforcement is complex. While the ultimate goal is internalization of achievement values, a great deal of internalizing by youngsters of this age cannot be expected, since many of them have had five years of not internalizing behind them. One thing that seems crucial is selectivity about what is reinforced. For example, in the beginning one might express approval for a simple act, such as a child's finding his own towel or returning it to the right hook. Later one should not emphasize approval for this, but rather for more difficult tasks.

Intellectual activities should be viewed in the same way, reinforcing the new thing tried, the difficult, the effort obviously expended, rather than applying reinforcement somewhat indiscriminately to any accomplishment of a task. Approval can be indicated also by attempting to throw it back to the child: "Aren't you proud of yourself that you could do so-and-so?"

With respect to concrete rewards, the question of what rewards tend to be more achievement-oriented, particularly school achievement-oriented, must be asked. From this standpoint, books, crayons, and paper are more appropriate than marbles and paddle balls. Unfortunately, they may also have lower reward value for culturally deprived children, and a balance between the two will have to be maintained. Symbolic rewards, progress charts, stars, and other outward and visible signs of an inward achievement should also be included.

3. The importance of the attitudinal aspects must be kept in mind. Training staffs associated with early training projects have tended to be highly achievement-oriented and inevitably the children sense this, either positively or negatively. Teachers need to be aware of their own attitudes toward achievement and to take steps to convey them to the child in a positive, deliberate manner rather than in a general and diffuse way. Through such awareness and by careful planning, competition can have a helpful effect upon the children. Setting realistic and clearly specified goals which the child can obtain in a relatively short period of time prevents the frustration of cumulative experiences of failure. Just as skills are developed in an orderly and sequential fashion, the

development of attitudes, such as motivation to achieve, follows an orderly and sequential pattern.

4. Some of the specific techniques we used in developing achievement motivation are the following:

(a) the stories told and read to the children. Time should be devoted to trying to collect story material directed toward achievement motivation with which the child may be able to identify. Also it is possible and desirable to develop original stories that illustrate achievements.

(b) concrete evidence of achievement which a child may keep and show to his parents. The youngsters should work over a period of several days to prepare booklets to take home. Anything of this kind should be capitalized upon and adapted to the range of ability evidenced by the members of the group.

(c) a record of the child's progress. Start a booklet for each child that would be a record of his personal progress week by week. This is easy to do in terms of color recognition and counting. It can also be done with copying designs—pegboards and the like. The booklet might also contain stars for conspicuous endeavor; these should be accompanied by a picture or symbol so that the child can, by referring to the booklet, tell what the star is for. This demands considerable hard work and ingenuity, but it can be one of the best techniques to help the child internalize and to compete with his past record. Such booklets can be used in an evaluation session once a week with small groups: "What has Helen learned this week? What is she going to try to learn next week?" This last question is designed to encourage the children to set standards of their own and to anticipate achievement.

(d) group activities directing the children toward competition with some standard—not necessarily, however, with each other. "How fast can you do this? How long can you do this? Can you do this new and difficult thing? Can you do as well as so-and-so?" It is well to think in terms of combining physical activity with such setting of competition motives, and usually it is more palatable, particularly with children who are much more physically oriented. Guessing games can also be used, thus contributing to language development at the same time.

Perhaps the chief thing to bear in mind is that most of the activities have, or can have, an achievement-oriented flavor. The problem is to make this explicit and to adjust it to each child's presumed level of competence and to the particular methods of handling him which seem appropriate.

DELAY OF GRATIFICATION

Delay of gratification is a term used to refer to the ability of an individual to postpone reward, to be willing to pass up immediate gain for a greater gain in the future. Both common sense and research would suggest that the ability to delay gratification is less characteristic of the culturally deprived child who usually comes from a home where people are almost by necessity forced to lead a hand-to-mouth existence. The pay check, or the welfare check, goes immediately to pay the rent and all the bills; what is left over must provide food for immediate needs and clothing needed at the immediate moment. On the other hand, planfulness and willingness to put off immediate pleasures for future gains tends to characterize a middle class group of people, whose present and future are more predictable, and who do not have all of their time and money drained into bare subsistence efforts.

We are not suggesting that we try to develop in our children the ability to delay gratification just to make them appear more like the middle class. This becomes a salient variable for intervention with deprived children simply because our whole pattern of education is such that only the individual who can delay immediate gratification has much chance of success. In simplest terms this means that the rewards for school-type activities are typically more delayed than immediate, and the child who is likely to achieve in school is one who is willing to put out some effort now to gain the social and self-approval that he may receive later on.

The problem is how to build up this ability to work for a deferred reward, or at least to make a start in this direction during the training period. The following conditions probably help in such a transition.

1. The child must have an environment and persons in it that can be trusted. Both the environment and the teacher must be

predictable. The teacher must never promise a reward and then neglect to give it to the child. One must be ever alert to reinforce the kind of behavior that one is attempting to develop.

2. The child must have numerous opportunities for a choice between immediate and delayed reward. These must be carefully planned so that the delayed reward is definitely more attractive to the child. Also, in beginning to help children learn to delay, the delays should not be great. In other words, one might first try to get the child to delay for an hour; toward the end of the training period, one might be able to get him to delay for two or three days.

3. One must help the child to see the consequences of being willing to delay gratification. For example, if one is starting out with the simple pattern of "one stick of candy now or two when we finish our work this hour," one must be sure that all the children who choose the immediate reward have a chance to observe the child who chooses the delayed reward when he finally gets his two sticks of candy.

4. At the time of the choice, one may reinforce the choice of a delayed reward showing liberal social approval of the child who chooses this. In other words, if Joe chooses to pass up a cookie now so that he can have a story book to take home, one should let the other children see that one approves of Joe's choice at the time he makes it.

One of the most important aspects of attempting to teach children to delay is setting the stage so that the child understands what one means by a little now or more later. Preschool children are typically rather young to comprehend this concept; one may have to try it out a number of times before the children really begin to see what one means by presenting the choice of a little now or more some time in the future.

PERSISTENCE

Persistence is so closely related to achievement motivation and to delay of gratification that it is hard to make meaningful distinctions and at the same time to avoid repeating material pertaining to those other variables. Nevertheless, our attempt will emphasize certain things we have tried to do to develop persistence toward a goal. Such persistence is a necessary condition for success in school activities and, indeed, in life as a whole.

In the beginning it is important to separate persistence from sheer perseveration—that is, continuing in a repetitive activity that has no particular goal in view. The child who sits in a swing for forty-five minutes, merely swinging back and forth, is not persisting, but simply perseverating. In teaching persistence, our first task was to find goals that were attractive enough to the children, and close enough to their capacities, that we could both encourage them to work toward the goal and also assure them of a fair chance of success. During the first summer, motor activities seemed particularly good for teaching persistence. The children already were more adept in motor skills than they were in most areas, so that the chances of accomplishment were somewhat greater. Also many motor activities are ones that provide a discernible end product; the child can ride the tricycle and knows when he has learned how to do it; he knows when he is at the top of the jungle gym; he knows when he has thrown the ball in the basket. The second task was to link goals that might have only weak attraction for the child with certain kinds of concrete reinforcement or social approval that had more salience for him.

An example of how we used these techniques is our teaching the children to throw a large ball into a wastebasket. After observing the children for a while, we made a rough estimate of how far the child could throw a ball accurately enough to have it land in the basket. With some children this was not more than two feet; there were other children who could throw it a distance of six or eight feet. Each child in the group was then encouraged to throw the ball from a distance just barely beyond his level of most likely success. He was kept at this task for a short period of time by the expression of adult approval for every time he tried. Much attention was paid to his successes, and all the children were encouraged to applaud when anyone made a successful throw.

Persistence in school-type tasks, such as working puzzles or learning to use crayons to color simple object drawings, was built up in a similar fashion, with the difference that concrete rewards were used more often in this case. Again, considerable care was used to see that the task provided for the child was one in which persistence for a reasonable amount of time would lead to reaching the goal.

If one looks at the probable environment of young deprived children, one characteristic of it is surely that persistence has not paid off. The environment is sufficiently disorganized, both spatially and from the standpoint of time schedules, that the child has difficulty in learning the sequences of events or the consequences of his acts. One characteristic approach of persons in deprived homes, from children to elderly people, seems to be an apathy that grows in part out of a feeling, often realistic, that the individual can achieve very little by his own efforts. He sees himself as being shaped by the environment rather than by being himself able to make changes in that environment.

In practical terms, this means that when one wants to promote persistence toward a goal in young deprived children, one must think in terms of having a clear and orderly environment that is highly predictable, one in which the child can see the consequences of his acts, and one in which the situation is so arranged that persisting toward a goal is followed by attaining the goal often enough so that the child learns that putting forth effort is likely to be rewarded.

DEVELOPING INTEREST IN SCHOOL-TYPE ACTIVITIES

One of our chief purposes was to attempt to bring children to the point where they found pleasure in the materials and activities similar to many of those to be expected in typical primary grades. The children came to summer school without the familiarity with the school-type items that are commonplace in middle class homes. They had no books, phonograph records, paper, pencils, crayons, paste, or scissors. One of our tasks was working with the children simply to show them how to use such materials appropriately. The children needed to learn how to hold pencils and crayons, how to cut with scissors, how to paste, and how to handle a book without completely endangering it.

A first task, then, was simply acquainting the child with such materials and encouraging him to explore their use. Therefore, in the beginning, we would give the child crayons and paper and encourage him to make marks on the paper. As he began, we tried to show him how to hold the crayon, using a very large one at the start. In the same way, looking at storybooks with him, we tried to show him how to turn the pages. The second task for us was the selection of materials, particularly books and records, close enough to the child's experience to tie in with his present interests.

Staff members were always available to help the youngsters learn to use such materials. In reading stories to the children, we found that the major determinant of the child's attention was probably the interest and skill displayed by the adult reading the story. For these children from three to four years old, reading stories demands a great deal more histrionic ability and more pointing out of objects in the pictures than might be needed with a middle class group.

Another general technique used in developing interest in school-type activities emphasized adult approval shown in the beginning by smiles and pats; later verbal approval was more frequently given.

Particularly with crayons, scissors, paste, and paper we developed materials for the children which they could complete and make into recognizable objects; these could be shown to the adults in the school and also to parents, as something accomplished by the children. As an illustration, an activity that was planned primarily to encourage the child in learning to classify objects by their use was one of going through old magazines to cut out pictures of what the child would like to eat for dinner. The pictures were gathered together and pasted on a sheet of paper. The children were encouraged to take their "dinners" home with them; the parents were primed for their arrival, with the hope that they would comment favorably upon the children's efforts.

A major project in developing products which indicate the children's facility with school-type materials was the record booklet that was prepared for each child at the end of the summer experience. These booklets were created to show how accomplished the child had become in performing certain tasks that were part of the summer preschool. On the first page of the record booklet, for example, were squares which could be colored in for each color that the child could name. There were also squares that could be checked in terms of the child's ability to count, with one check being made for every number he could actually count in sequence as he pointed out objects. The booklet also contained material on the number of songs the child knew, with little illustrations so that he could recognize the songs, material on storybooks that he was familiar with, and so on. These record booklets served to give the child some concrete evidence of his accomplishment, and, as expected, were employed by the home visitor in discussing with the mother the child's accomplishments over the summer.

IDENTIFICATION WITH ACHIEVING ROLE MODELS

Writers on culturally deprived children frequently point out that one of the major problems such children face, particularly little boys, is the absence of achieving role models with whom to indentify. This is especially true of role models whose achievements are in academic areas. The typical parents have had little schooling, and the probability is that older siblings of young deprived children will not themselves be models for achievement.

One of the things we noticed fairly early in the first summer was that the children watched adults and other children for cues as to what actions to make next. There was also some indication that the children guided their behavior by whatever the last person had done, if that individual had been approved for his behavior. One day we were trying to get the children to respond to verbal direction of behavior; we would hand one child a book and say, "John, put the book on the table." When John did put the book on the table, he was loudly approved. Then the next child was told, "Put the paper in the wastebasket, Sam." Sam went proudly and placed the paper on the table where John had placed the book. This tendency to imitate approved patterns of behavior suggests that the deprived child, perhaps even more than the middle class child, may profit by contact with role models who are achievement-oriented. In a sense, one might say that it is necessary to love children into taking on the patterns of attitudes and behavior that we were attempting to foster in our preschool.

Thus, the adults working with young deprived children should be ones who can serve as appropriate role models. This suggests that adults of both sexes should work in the preschool, and that some attention should be given to ethnic characteristics so that there is some compatibility with the children. Beyond this, the adults should self-consciously view themselves as identification figures and keep this in mind in such matters as their speech and the things for which they express interest and admiration. At the same time, they should remember that they have a major responsibility, not only in terms of being appropriate role models, but also in helping the children to go on to other situations, as inevitably they must.

We found, for example, that some of the fatherless little boys in our group formed very close attachments with the men; they felt that the adult males who took an interest in them as individuals were rare and wonderful. Such an identification may work wonders for a child while he is in a given group; if the child is not weaned away to some extent, however, from such identification, and encouraged to internalize somewhat his motivations, he may be expected to slip back once he is removed from the individual with whom he has been identifying.

Perhaps it is helpful at this point to make a distinction between role identification and emotional identification. Presumably role identification consists of patterning one's behavior after that of the individual with whom one has identified, without necessarily experiencing the strong emotional tie that may exist between one individual and another with whom he is closely identified. Father-figures are needed and are important for such young children, but it is important always to remember that the child must make an emotional transition to other individuals. Thus preschool teachers and assistants should make efforts to encourage children to use them as role models, but at the same time should be cautious about encouraging strong emotional identification.

II

APTITUDES RELATED TO ACHIEVEMENT

Perception, concept development, and language were three major aptitude variables with which we worked in the Early Training Project. These variables are obviously interrelated, particularly in the methods we used to improve the children's ability to perceive more precisely, to broaden their range of concepts and their facility in ordering their world, and to develop their language comprehension and usage to a more effective level.

There are times when the distinctions between the variables relating to attitude and those relating to aptitude become somewhat hazy. In other words, the motivations of the child are of major importance in developing his ability to make perceptual discriminations, to extend the range of adequacy of his concepts, and to improve his language comprehension and usage. Thus, the improvement of aptitudes related to achievement was aided by developing motivation to achieve, to persist toward a goal, to delay gratification, and by identifying with role models who were themselves facile in making fine perceptual discriminations and in using language. For our present purposes we shall treat each of these three aptitude variables separately, although the reader should remember that the boundaries between them are at times imprecise.

THE DEVELOPMENT OF PERCEPTION

Perception may be thought of in simple terms as the recognition or identification of patterns of sensory stimulation. We perceive a pencil when a certain pattern of light waves gives us sensations of color as yellow, and of form as elongated with a single, pointed end. We perceive an apple through still other patterns of color and shape, as well as odor and taste. It is tremendously important for the child's effective learning in school and life that he be able to recognize and label a large range of object and events. The ability to make differential perceptions—to see how objects or events are alike or different—is the very basis upon which school learning is built. Reading, for example, demands among other abilities that of making precise discriminations between an *n* and an *m*; he must literally know his *p*'s and *q*'s.

The culturally deprived child will usually exhibit two kinds of deficiencies in the area of perception. First, he will often be unable to discriminate between two objects or events that are highly similar. For example, the deprived child may have some difficulty distinguishing between the two figures shown here:

The disadvantaged child is not likely to see the difference in the placement of the rabbit's ears. If one examines the probable home life of the deprived child, it is not difficult to see the origin of this deficiency. His home will tend to be cramped and overcrowded it will probably be relatively disorganized, both the arrangement of objects within it, and also in time sequences; his home often has no clock, no regular time for meals, no usual bedtime—those standing patterns of events common to the middle class home. This lack of order means a vagueness and diffuseness of structure in his surroundings in which the child cannot well perceive the relevant aspects of a situation which pertains to making discriminations. How can he see in what ways cooking pans are alike or different if the two are lying in a welter of a dozen other objects, rather than hanging side by side on hooks?

Although the deprived home will have much in the way of sensory stimulation within it, the range of different objects and events will tend to be rather restricted. There is always a great deal of noise, but in a sense it is the same old noise. There are many things to look at in the crowded room, but they are the same things day after day. The advantaged child, on the other hand, probably has within his home a much wider range of objects, many consciously provided for him, such as his own story books and his own crayons and paper. He also comes into contact with far more objects and situations outside the home and his immediate neighborhood; he is the child who goes on family vacations and other trips, who goes with his mother to the library, the supermarket, and the children's museum.

Our efforts in the Early Training Project to increase the child's perceptual development employed two approaches. First, we provided a number of situations in which the children were enabled to make precise discriminations and encouraged to do so. The section on activities describes many of the materials we used, such as beads, pegs, blocks (differing in size, shape, and color), pictures, and puzzles. In general, our approach was one of presenting materials a few at a time, in a situation that was not distracting either visually or in terms of sound, and of encouraging the child to distinguish as many aspects of the object or picture as he could. While reading stories to the children, for example, the teacher would point out the picture that illustrated the story and would encourage the children to talk about what was in the picture: "Which is Baby Bear's bed?" or, "Which house did the third little pig build?" In looking at fruits, in touching them, smelling them, and eating bites of them, the children were again encouraged to notice the qualities of each particular fruit.

Our second way of approaching the improvement of perceptual ability was focused on extending the range of objects and situations which the child learned to recognize. Wherever possible we started with objects and events that occurred naturally in their environment but to which they apparently had not given attention previously. We tried to present many common sounds to them for recognition, using a tape recorder—the sound of a car, a truck, a train, a ball bouncing, an eggbeater twirling, and so on. We encouraged the children to bring to the group different kinds of leaves, flowers, insects, and feathers. We started with the naturally available objects and situations, for we hoped thereby to have more carryover into the child's everyday living. If we could get him to the point of noticing likeness and differences in the birds of the community, or the flowers, or the sounds made by different kinds of vehicles, he could continue to expand his perceptual world. For this world, although somewhat limited in potential, is by no means so limited as is the use the deprived child often makes of it. One point of caution was observed in all this "enriching" of the environment: we took care that the child was not presented with a large number of objects at one time or in such close sequence that he was hurried in exploring their characteristics or qualities.

In all of our attempts to heighten the perceptual development of the child, we assumed that by whatever means seemed appropriate, we must move the child from a passive approach to new situations and objects to one of active exploration. In the beginning, many of the children needed encouragement to explore new objects—to pick them up and handle them, and to shake them. They needed enthusiastic support as they tried to string wooden beads according to a given sequence, or to build up a color cone in the proper order. We attempted to promote this active exploration by supporting the child as he embarked on new activities and by the liberal use of physical reward (bodily contact) or verbal approval for his behavior.

CONCEPTUAL DEVELOPMENT

As we suggested in the introduction to this section, it is not easy to know where percepts leave off and where concepts begin. It is also hard to draw fine lines between conceptual and linguistic development, since once the child acquires adequate language, much of the abstracting required to develop new concepts is done by way of verbalization.

For our purposes we may define the learning of concepts as the acquiring or using of a common response or label for two or more completely identical objects or stimuli. Thus, the child learns to call both the beagle and the collie, *dog;* to say that both the apple and the stop sign are *red.* In both these cases, we might say that common qualities are abstracted for the two nonidentical objects. In the case of the beagle and the collie, it is easy to see how the child may be led on to more inclusive concepts; there are also spaniels, terriers, bird dogs. He may be led to understand concepts on a higher level; dogs are animals, animals are living things, and so on. This use of abstraction at all levels is one of the most important tools the middle class child brings to school, and one of those most in demand in contemporary western civilization.

For many already familiar reasons the home situation of the deprived child makes adequate concept development difficult. His environment is not only marked by a lack of stimulating materials relevant to later school achievement, but by spatial and temporal disorganization that makes the discovery of common qualities among objects difficult. In the home, for example, where clothing is kept neatly sorted as to type—shirts, shorts, socks—and sorted according to a particular wearer, the child can learn such concepts as clothing appropriate for a small boy, for a mother, for a big girl, for winter wear, for dress-up wear, and so on. Where all the clothes are jumbled together, the abstracting of common characteristics is far more difficult. In addition, the more restricted range of objects means that the child has fewer opportunities to classify and order his world. If his mother has only three cooking pans, it is not likely that he can develop concepts of skillets, saucepans, and cake tins, or can learn to classify all of these as cooking utensils.

The environment of the culturally deprived child is also language-poor. Here, again, he has few adult models, and those he has are usually not willing to talk with him in any detail, particularly in order to help him label his environment or to assist him in abstracting common qualities from the objects within it. Most often his language models are his peers or his brothers and sisters. Practically, this results in the child's concepts remaining largely on a simple, functional level. All young children will define a chair as something to sit in, but this sort of concrete functional usage persists much longer in the deprived child than in the advantaged one. Such a concrete conceptual world is appropriate to primitive societies, but it is highly inefficient in a world that demands of each person the ability to order a wide range of varying stimuli and to seek their similarities and differences.

The ability to abstract common qualities is particularly crucial when we consider one of the major ways in which the child builds up a stable picture of his world; that way is through finding constancies, unvarying or regular relationships between objects and events, including cause and effect. The disorganized home of the deprived child is a poor place to find constancies. They exist, but in the general welter the child cannot find them. The advantaged child may learn, for example, that ice melts if you put an ice cube in a warm room; he also learns that it melts slowly, unless you put it on the stove. To learn this, however, demands that the ice cube stays in one place for a certain length of time, and that you are not distracted by other events so much that you cannot attend to the relations between the warm room and the melting of the ice. The middle class child learns that if you break a candy bar in two, you have just as much candy as you had before. But this learning presupposes again that the candy stays around a little while—you can occasionally wait to eat your candy without the danger that someone else will take it away, or that it will get misplaced in the general confusion.

In the Early Training Project we made concerted efforts to set up an environment for the children that was predictable, organized, and rich enough in objects and situations that it was possible for the child to learn to order his world. Thus, he could begin to focus upon both the physical and interpersonal dimensions of the training program that were relevant to his cognitive development. We emphasized number concepts, color concepts, and other concepts concerning the most familiar aspects of the child's world. We attempted to expand the child's world in both breadth and depth. From the relatively few foodstuffs he knew, for instance, we could broaden the categories by giving him experiences of seeing, tasting, and handling other new foods of a particular class. Further, each example could be classified as vegetables, fruit, grain, meat, or cheese; later, vegetables could be classified as those that grew above or below the ground. The opportunities to classify foods by color and to count the items in a class provided an exercise in using these concepts meaningfully.

During the first summer of the Early Training Project we were particularly concerned with developing color and number concepts. We were also concerned with developing in the children the ability to sort objects by common characteristics, such as putting together all the things that are round, those that are red, those you can eat, those you can wear, and the like. Later we attempted to teach the children position concepts (behind, above, or inside), action categories (running, walking, or hopping), and simple time concepts.

In this area, as well as in our efforts to extend the range of the child's perception and to increase his ability to discriminate, we also tried to use examples from the child's own environment. For example, wherever possible the children first learned about fruit and vegetables from those growing or being sold in the community; later we moved out to include some of the more exotic varieties of fruit found in the supermarket or flowers found in picture books. We related colors, numbers, clothing, and furniture, to the objects in their home environments. This again was an effort to provide a continuity with the home so that the child would have an opportunity at home to rehearse some of the things to which he was being exposed in the school situation.

LANGUAGE DEVELOPMENT

It is extremely hard to draw neat distinctions between language development and concept formation, or even between language development and perceptual development. Piaget, for example, takes the approach that the child's language is primarily the way in which the child is able to test out the reality of his own perceptions and the generalizations he makes from them, that is, his concepts. Thus he comes to use verbal signs which other persons use, and from our standpoint, then becomes "teachable."

Because of the home backgrounds of culturally deprived children, we may expect them to be retarded in verbal development, sometimes severely so. There is some evidence that culturally deprived children will tend to be even more retarded in spoken language than they are in understood language. This may be the function of a home which has perhaps depended more on emotional communication, which can be effected through gesture, expression, and tone of voice, than upon more abstract or intellectual communication, which almost always has to be expressed through words. Verbal communication may also be dependent upon the presence of adults who positively encourage the child to talk, to learn to label his world, and to respond verbally to adult speech. Evidence seems to suggest that it is not so much by simply listening to the speech of others that the child acquires verbal skills, as it is by his attempts to respond to their verbal productions and his being rewarded for these efforts. This may be the reason why watching television apparently does little to stimulate language development of the culturally deprived.

We live in a world where language is our most effective means of communicating. Schoolwork tends to be highly verbal in nature. If we hope for any success for our children in school, we must improve their general language development. Every opportunity should be taken to set the stage so that it is necessary for the child to use language to reach the goal he wants. When the children are playing with wheel toys, for example, one should supervise closely enough to see that the child can obtain the wheel toy he wants from another child only by asking for it. One can also in the same way teach the child that certain kinds of language tend to be effective ways of getting what they want. If a child wants to ride the tricycle, one can suggest that he first ask the child already riding it for a turn as soon as the first child is through. The lunch hour is also an excellent time to encourage using complete sentences and learning names of new foods.

A second general rule is directly reinforcing the child for language productivity. For example, if Joe speaks in a complete sentence, he gets a piece of candy; if he says "red" rather than, "The apple is red," he does not get one. Social reinforcement may be used in the same way and perhaps more frequently.

Another important procedure is the teacher's taking time to listen to the child's verbal productions. To have an adult get down on their level physically and listen intently to what they say can be a very reinforcing experience for these youngsters, many of whom have few opportunities to obtain the attentive ear of an older person.

The following are several ways of encouraging language production on the part of the children.

1. Encourage the children to relate their own experiences about simple activities. Ask them what they had for breakfast that day, what they like best for dinner, what they saw on the way to school.

2. Provide experiences for the children and then discuss them together. Take them on a walk to see anything that is new on the school ground. If a new flower opens, take the children out to see it. When the group returns, they can talk about it, and several children can contribute.

3. "A secret in the sack" is a familiar technique used by primary teachers which can be simplified and adapted for use with preschool children. Put a simple, easily identified, object (an orange perhaps) in a paper bag. The children are allowed to touch it, smell it, and then asked to identify it. Ask them how they knew it was an orange, or whatever. Objects used for this purpose should be easy for children to identify—such as fruit, a piece of Kleenex, a pocket comb, a pencil, or a book.

4. Frequent reading of stories and *talking about them* is one of the best techniques. Skillful use of stories for language development takes a good bit of preparation and practice, but the preparation pays off in the increased attention of the children.

5. If a tape recorder is available, use it with some of the techniques already discussed, such as accounts of the children's own experiences. The playback of their own voices will serve to stimulate them to further conversations. It would also be a good idea to do a tape recording of the youngsters' voices early in the training period and then to file it away for comparison of their language development at a later date.

7. The more advanced children can probably do simple dramatizations of familiar stories. A few basic props such as squares

of cloth for capes and skirts, and various kinds of headgear can heighten the effect for youngsters.

8. Puppets may be used to stimulate language development. Children will spontaneously use the puppets for biting one another's fingers; this probably releases a little hostility, but does nothing to promote language development. Encourage the children to have the puppets speak to one another, and with the more advanced children, invite them to act out simple dramas with the puppets.

9. The ability to follow directions is not only a good test of language comprehension but it is something which may be built up systematically by giving the child directions beginning with a simple single command and giving him somewhat more complex directions and additional commands as his ability increases. Thus, we start with, "Put the book on the table," and many actions of this sort. Then go on to, "Pick the book up off the chair and put it on the table," and even later to, "Put the book on the table and bring me the pencil that is on the desk." You can easily work out a game with youngsters by giving each one a different command and encouraging some competition among them to see who can respond most quickly—and correctly—to this command.

You must be ever on the alert to reinforce the children's language productivity. This means taking time to listen to what they are saying and praising them or rewarding them concretely for improved language usage. Also, as suggested at the beginning of this section, the teacher should set the stage so that the use of language enables the child to reach the goal towards which he is striving. If you can make the use of language a rewarding experience for the child, you can expect him to talk more, and more adequately.

IV

ACTIVITIES DESIGNED TO IMPLEMENT THE PROGRAM

The purpose of this chapter is to present a relatively detailed account of the day-by-day activities of the summer program. Its emphasis is on the *why* and *how* rather than the *what* of the materials. That is, this chapter attempts to show why particular activities were selected and how they were carried out in relation to the attitude and aptitude variables previously discussed.

MATERIALS AND ACTIVITIES RELATED TO LANGUAGE, CONCEPTS, AND PERCEPTS

The child's ability to focus upon the relevant dimensions of the tasks he performs in school is related to his perceptual ability and his level of concept development. He must be able to distinguish a variety of forms, colors, and numbers. His senses must function adequately in order to discriminate what is important from what is extraneous to the task. His small muscles must be coordinated so that he can cope with the demands of reading and writing. School activities demand particular visual, auditory, and kinesthetic perceptual skills which must be learned. If he is to be successful in meeting these demands, the child must also have an adequate repertory of concepts built on experience. Language provides the means to manipulate his environment abstractly without resorting to trial-and-error physical responses.

The materials and activities presented in this section are designed to develop the child's perceptual, conceptual, linguistic, and motor skills by furnishing opportunities to manipulate interesting and attractive objects purposefully. The first experience the child has with these materials, many of which are completely new to him, is one of orientation. His initial reaction is primitive; he responds to them with the only actions he knows—throwing, scrambling, and the like. It is necessary that he have his initial experience in small groups where the group leader can provide tasks that the child can complete successfully. Later, as he discovers the possibilities the materials offer, he can be allowed more independence in his work. Initially the teacher provides immediate and material reward for his efforts; gradually, the reinforcement shifts from material reward to social approval. The teacher also moves from reinforcement for every successful completion of a task to a more intermittent schedule of reward.

As the child learns and finds success in the first simple activities, he will want to continue them; then the teacher plans more complex tasks which stretch his ability and challenge his ingenuity. Careful and varied choice from a broad selection of activities helps to keep his interest and motivation at a high level; but most of all, successful experiences help to develop persistence. While some children will persist longer at a task than others, this quality can be developed in each child. Obtaining desired rewards and receiving the approval of important adults are effective ways of reinforcing persistent behavior.

Picture file. The development of an extensive picture file as an aid to language and concept development is essential. Describing events and objects in a picture can stimulate language fluency and development, and the association of pictorial events with real experiences aids the ability to abstract. Reading a picture takes skill; the child must learn to differentiate figure from ground. Black and white as well as color pictures should be included. He must learn that important objects usually appear larger toward the bottom of the picture or overlapping other objects. Density and convergence must be recognized as cues to distance. Discovering relationships, interpreting motion, and appreciating aesthetic qualities are skills which can be developed with pictures.

Picture puzzles. Picture puzzles, made from duplicate pictures of those in the file, mounted on heavy tag board and then cut up, provide an opportunity for the child to test his ability to reconstruct his initial experiences with the pictorial materials. The activity serves to reinforce his efforts and to permit the teacher to assess areas that need more development.

Picture sequences. Series of pictures that can be arranged in sequence are useful. Here the child learns to move from event to event developing time and sequence concepts. The theme, for example, of *The Three Bears* can be reconstructed after the story has been read. Some picture sequences are available commercially; others can be made by someone who can do simple sketches, for example, of a bird starting to build a nest, completing it, incubating eggs, hatching eggs, feeding the young, and so on. With preschool children you might well begin with only two pictures to be placed in proper sequence, then gradually build up to a greater number. Practice and encouragement in developing the ability to place such pictures in a meaningful time sequence is particularly important for deprived children, since in general their home environment does not stress orderly sequences of events.

Picture sorting. Groups of pictures belonging to classes with sub-classes can be sorted again and again according to the concepts relevant at the moment. For instance, food, animals, clothing, and furniture provide many opportunities for such sorting. Food pictures can be sorted into vegetable, fruit, meat, dairy products, etc., and further sub-classes can be developed such as root vegetables, leafy vegetables, seed vegetables. Furniture can be classified according to the appropriate room in the household. It can be further sorted according to use. These sorting tasks are directed at concept development, but are built upon perceptual skills and provide many opportunities for language development.

Jig-saw puzzles. Jig-saw puzzles are available in series which are graded for difficulty; the Sifo puzzles are an example. Some commercial series are available which show the inner workings of an important part when the piece is removed; for instance, removal of the beehive uncovers a picture of the inner activity.

The simplest puzzles provide training in form and color discrimination and simple eye–hand coordination. The child must match the form pieces to the appropriate holes, using the color cues that are provided. As his skill develops, puzzles are introduced in which complete objects, vegetables, fruits, or animals, are placed in the appropriate spaces; later, important parts of an object must be fitted together in order to produce the whole. A puzzle in which each piece is a meaningful part of the whole will be more valuable than one consisting of randomly cut parts, since to put together one of the former, the child must focus on the meaning and relationship of the different pieces. An animal which has been cut into body, head, legs, feet, and tail is meaningfully assembled according to relevant features of the animal. Extension of this experience to developing the concept of functional use of parts is possible. Unfortunately, many puzzles are not too well planned in this respect. Teacher-made puzzles, although inferior technically, may well be superior for learning concepts, particularly the concept of relationships. A large picture of a head mounted on a heavy poster board, and then cut into meaningful parts—eyes, nose, ears, forehead, mouth and chin—will demand close attention to what is pictured on the puzzle piece, and to the relationships of the parts.

Pegboards. Pegboards, nine inches square, used with a large assortment of colored pegs, are particularly helpful in developing spatial orientation, such as left to right, and top to bottom. Such an aid also encourages the development of persistence, fine motor control, and the ability to follow visual patterns and aural directions. Training begins with simple designs constructed in the child's presence by the teacher; "First we'll make a line of blue pegs across the top. We start here (indicating the top left hand corner)." Continuous reinforcement is supplied as the child chooses the correct color and moves along in his construction. When he successfully completes the line he is rewarded materially for his efforts. Opportunities to develop positional concepts incidental to the pegboard designs form an important part of the activity. As a simple square (box) is made, two red apples (pegs) can be placed inside the box, and so forth. Many variations on this theme are possible and the children can be given the opportunity to give directions for others to follow.

As skills develop, more complex designs can be introduced accompanied by models for the child to follow. Models are made on a piece of paper divided into a grid by light lines. Pegs are represented by large colored dots in the squares. As the designs increase in complexity the teacher can reward persistent effort and the completion of the design. The child can make small replicas of his designs to keep and exhibit as he completes each one in a graded series.

The next three pages illustrate possible pegboard designs useful in developing some of the skills mentioned in this section, along with some of the concepts that may be developed with each of the designs.

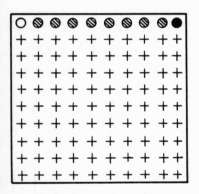

I. Horizontal line
   Concepts stressed:
   a. left to right
   b. start—green, stop—red
   c. counting: 1–10
   d. colors: red, green, blue
   e. repeat design, middle, bottom.

II. Vertical line
   Concepts stressed:
   a. top to bottom
   b. start—green, stop—red
   c. counting: 1–10
   d. colors: red, green, yellow
   e. repeat design, middle, right side.

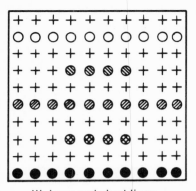

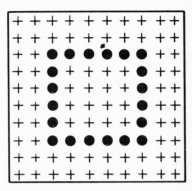

III. Long and short lines
Concepts stressed:
a. short, long
b. between, beginning, ending
c. counting
d. colors: red, green, yellow, blue, purple

IV. Closed box
Concepts stressed:
a. square, top, bottom, sides
b. around, closed
c. inside, outside

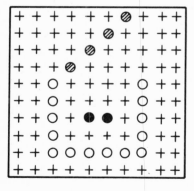

V. Open box
Concepts stressed:
a. lid, open
b. slant, angle
c. inside

VI. Stairs
Concepts stressed:
a. downstairs, upstairs
b. foot, tread, riser
c. zig-zag
d. counting

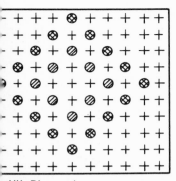

VII. Diamonds
   Concepts stressed:
   a. small, large
   b. inside, outside,
      middle, around

VIII. Interlocking squares
   Concepts stressed:
   a. top, bottom, sides
   b. next to
   c. cross

Color cones and beads. The color cone consists of large, brightly colored wooden doughnuts placed on a peg according to color or size. It may be used to emphasize the learning of such concepts as largest, larger, smaller, smallest, as well as color discrimination. It is a valuable device for beginning work, and for the slower, more immature children in order to provide success experiences.

Stringing beads offers many opportunities for following directions, discriminating three-dimensional forms, and developing a sequence. The end product can be worn as a reward, especially by the girls, although the boys often enjoy this as well. Persisting in the development of a complex pattern in which one must attend likeness and differences in size, shape, and color of the beads can be encouraged. In developing his string, the child has repeated opportunities to count, as he relates his production to the pattern in a one-to-one relationship.

One-inch cubes. School supply stores stock one-inch wooden cubes, both in natural finish and in colors, which we found to be useful in a number of ways. Achievement motivation and persistence could be encouraged by working with the children in build-

ing various structures. The tower could be made higher, or t
house more elaborate as the child progressed in ability. The cut
were also useful for counting, for color recognition, and for use
teaching position concepts. Some illustrations of ways in whi
cubes may be used are given on the following two pages.

I.
Build one three-color tower.

"Which block is *up*?"
"Which block is *down*?"

Rebuild in different color
order, direct questions to
specific children and their
towers.

"Which block is in the
middle?"
"Which block is on *top*?"
"Which block is on the
bottom?"

Each child builds his tower
according to directions.

"Put the yellow block *be-
neath* the red one."
"Put the blue block *on top of*
the red one."
"Take the blue block *from*
the top."

II.
Build two single-color trains.

"Put the yellow train *in
front of* the red train."

"Put the yellow train *behind*
the red train."
"Put a yellow smokestack
on top of the red train," etc.

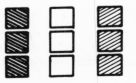

III.
Build three one-color towers.

"Put the yellow tower *between* the red and blue
towers."

Rebuild according to directions.

''First build a yellow tower.
Then build a red tower *beside* the yellow tower.''

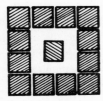

V.
Build two one-color towers
plus one blue block.

''Move the red tower *to-
ward* the yellow tower.''
''Move the yellow tower
away from the red tower.''
''Move the blue block *over*
the two towers.''
''Put the blue block *be-
tween* the two towers.''

''Build a blue tower *beside*
the red one. Now put the
yellow tower in the *middle*.''

IV.
Place twelve red blocks in a
rectangle plus one blue
block.

''Put the blue block *into* the
red square.''
''Put the blue block in the
middle of the space.''
''Put the blue block *outside*
the red square.''
''Put the blue block *inside*
the red square.''

cardboard

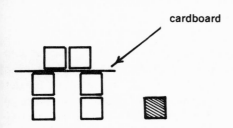

VI.
Build one six-block bridge
with a piece of cardboard
plus o ne blue block.
''Put the blue block *under-
neath* the bridge,'' etc.

Flannel boards. With a little ingenuity the flannel board can be used effectively to tell stories. The children are entranced as the story unfolds both in the telling and visual development. Taking turns both in telling the story and placing the objects on the board is a rewarding experience. There are many other uses for this device; the opportunities are not limited to flannel cutouts since pictures can be backed with small pieces of flannel or sandpaper so that they will adhere to the board. Language development can be stimulated with a series of sequential pictures. Each child is given a picture and as he tells his part of the story he puts it in place. The teacher can arrange them in scrambled order for the child to rearrange as he is telling the story. Using the small flannel cutouts available through supply houses one is equipped to teach concepts involving size, shape, number, color, relationships and position.

Counting frame and dominoes. For developing concepts of numbers and groups both of these pieces of equipment are useful. The counting frame, made of beads strung on wires, is used for counting and grouping. Toward the end of the training period the more able child may even be able to use the beads in counting by two's. Matching number groups on large dominoes develops group concepts. The child can be rewarded for his matching efforts as he makes his "number road."

Magnifying glass. Large and small magnifying glasses capture the interest of children quickly. We found that the type of magnifying glass which rests upon a tripod has been of greatest value in the Early Training Project. The children can place all manner of objects under such an instrument for closer scrutiny. The opportunities are endless for exploring natural phenomena, insects, ants, grass, shells, parts of animals, seeds, and leaves. The children will spend long periods of time just looking at their hands, comparing and contrasting size, counting fingers, looking at "hurts" and blemishes, that is, discriminating differences and noticing similarities.

SPECIFIC SMALL GROUP ACTIVITIES
TESTED AND USED EFFECTIVELY

1. Visual Skills:

    a. *Size and Form*

Purpose:	To develop visual discrimination skills.
Materials:	Circles, squares, and rectangles of various sizes.
Procedure:	Child arranges in sequence according to size or form (different sizes of pictures of toys and animals can be used, as well as objects).

    b. *Matching Shapes*

Purpose:	To develop visual discrimination skills.
Materials:	Mimeo or ditto sheets divided into halves, top half in quarters.
Procedure:	Forms on bottom half of sheet are cut, matched, and pasted to forms at top half of paper. Forms may be colored according to key.

    c. *Form Bingo*

Purpose:	To develop visual discrimination skills.
Materials:	Tagboard ruled into sixteen three-inch squares. On each square a form or picture is permanently fixed. All cards are the same. An extra set is made for the instructor cut into individual stimulus (S) cards.
Procedure:	S cards are held up by the teacher, child places bead over his matching forms or picture (children's cards are the same but pictures are in different sequences).

    d. *What's Missing?*

Purpose:	To develop visual discrimination skills.

Materials: Large pictures mounted on tagboard with
              one important part missing. Envelopes con-
              taining missing parts.

Procedure: Child finds missing part and places it in
              proper place; or, leader holds up picture,
              child who can guess missing part by name gets
              to find it and place it on picture.

e. *Change the Circle*

Purpose: To develop visual discrimination skills.

Materials: Chalkboard, chalk.

Procedure: Leader places large circle on board. Children
              cover their eyes. Leader places line through
              circle. Child who can tell what has been
              changed is rewarded.

f. *Matching Pictures*

Purpose: To develop visual discrimination skills.

Materials: Two sets of like pictures of objects such as
              a card, hat, or cup.

Procedure: Leader deals all the cards in one set to the chil-
              dren with about five or six cards to each. Then
              the leader holds up one card at a time from
              the second set. The child who has the match
              takes the card. The one who matches up his
              five or six cards first wins.

Variation: Shapes and numbers may also be used.

2. Auditory Skills:

a. *Sound Alikes*

Purpose: To develop discrimination skills.

Materials: Series of riddles, e.g., "I rhyme with (sound
              like) sled, you sleep in me, what am I?"

Procedure: Leader asks rhyme riddle, rewards correct
              response with token; tokens turned in at end
              of period for reward.

b. *Rhyming Words*

Purpose: To develop skills in categorization by auditory similarities

Materials: Stimulus pictures: house, eye, clown, fire. Response pictures: mouse, pie, town, tire.

Procedure: Each child is given a stimulus (S) picture and chooses a response (R) picture which goes with his S picture. Since matching the pictures is only a physical response, be sure that the child says the words that apply to his pictures so that he can hear the auditory similarities in the rhymes.

3. Kinesthetic Skills:

a. *Surprise Box*

Purpose: To develop skills in description using kinesthetic cues.

Materials: Box of objects of different sizes shapes and textures—comb, tooth brush, bottle cap, crayon, emery board, handkerchief blindfold.

Procedure: Child is blindfolded and asked to draw an object out of the box. Leader asks such questions as: "Is it hard or soft?" "Is it large or small?" Many descriptive ideas are encouraged before leader lets child tell what he thinks the item is.

4. Concept Development:

a. *Animal Frolic*

Purpose: To develop categorization and discrimination skills.

Materials: Pictures of barnyard, zoo, circus, forest, house. Small pictures of animals, dog, duck, goat, chick, tiger, elephant.

Procedure: Child sorts animals according to the category. Series is made up with one that does not belong; child chooses the one that does not belong.

b. *Going Shopping*

Purpose: To develop skill in memorizing complex visual stimulus.

Materials: Empty boxes, cartons, cans, and other food containers on shelf; shopping bag per child. Collage of pictures pasted on list. Begin with three pictures, increasing gradually for greater difficulty of task.

Procedure: Child is permitted to study card for short period, then goes shopping without card to get all articles on "list."

Variation: Many possible with this. Pick all the vegetables which grow above the ground. Pick the vegetable that sounds like "meat."

c. *Find My Mother*

Purpose: To encourage growth in the concept of development.

Materials: Two sets of pictures, one of baby animals, one of adult animals.

Procedure: Child is asked to match baby animal with its mother.

d. *Peg It*

Purpose: To develop skill in color discrimination and in using quantitative concepts.

Materials: Set of color and number cards for each child (cards have string loop at one end). Peg board with peg for each child.

Procedure: Each child is given a set of cards. As he identifies each card he hangs it on his peg on the board. The child who has the most cards on his peg is the winner.

e. *Belonging Together*

Purpose: To increase comprehension development.

Materials: Pictures or objects in several familiar categories such as toys, animals, foods.

Procedure: Leader displays objects and asks children to pick up (or point to) only the things to eat, only the things that run on wheels.

5. **Language Development:**

a. *Picture Stories*

Purpose: To increase use of descriptive adjectives.

Materials: Pictures of animals doing tricks, eating, playing.

Procedure: Leader shows pictures and asks such questions as, "What is the dog doing?" "How does he feel?" "What does his hair feel like?"

b. *Tell About Me*

Purpose: To develop descriptive vocabulary (language fluency).

Materials: None.

Procedure: In turn, each child stands. The other children each give one descriptive idea about the child who is standing, such as, "Bobby has on brown pants." "Bobby has short hair."

c. *Telling a Story*

Purpose: To develop sequences and language fluency.

Materials: Sets of pictures that tell a story in sequence.

Procedure: Ask child to arrange pictures so that they tell a story. Have child tell story.

d. *I Am Wishing*

Purpose: To develop a descriptive and functional vocabulary.

Materials: Empty show box. Set of cards with toy pictures, airplane, ball, bicycle, blocks, boat, bunny, cars, engine, hammer, scooter.

Procedure: Each child is given about three cards. Leader
              says, "I am wishing for a toy that bounces."
              Child with proper picture deposits it in box
              and is rewarded.
Variation: Instead of functional definitions use descrip-
              tive definitions, for example, "I wish for a
              toy that's red, round, and smooth." Reverse
              process to get child to give description.

6. Social Concepts:

   a. *Who Am I, What Do I Do?*

      Purpose: To develop skills in social recognition.
      Materials: Pictures of community helpers, postman, gro-
                  cer, policemen, dentist, garbage collector.
      Procedure: Leader holds up picture, children guess who
                  each one is and tell what he does.

7. Sensory Experience:

   a. *Surprise Box*

      Purpose: To develop kinesthetic discrimination—sen-
                  sory experience.
      Materials: Objects of different textures in cigar box,
                  sponge, piece of sandpaper, smooth satin,
                  piece of fur, piece of velvet, cotton.
      Procedure: Each child takes turn with closed eyes and
                  describes his object, guesses material.

   b. *Smell Box*

      Purpose: To develop olfactory discrimination—sensory
                  experience.
      Materials: Items chosen from spice rack, cinnamon
                  sticks, nutmeg, sage; or from bathroom toi-
                  letries, toilet water, soap, toothpaste.
      Procedure: Each child takes turn with closed eyes and
                  describes what he smells, then guesses sub-
                  stance.

c. *Taste Box*

Purpose: To develop taste discrimination—sensory experience.

Materials: Household seasonings in box, salt, sugar, alum, vinegar, mouthwash.

Procedure: Turns are taken with closed eyes and child describes taste, guesses material.

MUSIC, RECORDS, AND RHYTHMS

This section is concerned with singing, singing games, rhythm band, and rhythmic activities, and listening to music—piano, records, tape recordings. Some of the items included are not strictly "music," but are described here because of their resemblance to some of the other items discussed.

These activities were used not only to give the children musical experiences but also to promote the aptitude and attitude variables with which the Early Training Project has been concerned. Thus, singing was used to encourage language and also concept development; listening was directed toward sound discrimination. The activities also were related to the attitudinal variables, especially in the choice of the various items we used and of the way in which the teacher worked with the children to develop competence in singing and in the use of rhythm band instruments.

Musical activities provide one of the most powerful tools in developing language use because music places language in an enjoyable and satisfying context. For the young culturally disadvantaged child whose language development is retarded and who lacks verbal skills to hold his own independently in any discussion, music affords the opportunity to participate with the group and offers, as well, the shelter of group response to hide his inadequacies until such time as he can express himself freely. While at times the child may be observed in communication with his peers, in the presence of adult authority figures he is unlikely to risk exposure by employing a skill in which he is so inadequate. Singing offers the sustained verbal practice in forming speech patterns and word associations that the child needs. He enjoys the repetition which, without the rhythmic involvement and variable intonation, would be a boring exercise. The combination of music, rhythm, and words calls for a total emotional, physical, and cognitive response, thus maximizing stimulation through several senses. Music also has a strong element of predictability; the child constantly experiences temporal organization and the predictability of sequence in the words as well as music. Musical activities require the child to pay attention not only to learn new tunes and words when they are initially presented, but also to anticipate the actions or words that come next in a learned tune. Developing the skills of listening and being alert to the variety of cues necessary in oral communication are encouraged in musical activities.

Music activities afford the opportunity for a shared experience in which the concept of interdependence is strong. In using rhythm instruments, the group is dependent upon the strong beat of the bass drum; the chime of the triangle and the clash of the cymbals on cue. The child learns to be a cooperative member of the group through his contribution to the group effort.

If available, an accompanist is a valuable asset to the teacher in presenting new material. This frees the teacher to give her undivided attention to the vocalization and movements the song demands. Often a volunteer is available to help with this portion of the program. If the teacher is skilled in playing an instrument, all the better; if not, other aids in the form of records and tape recordings are available.

Group singing. Group singing in which the songs are learned by rote, develops in children the ability to listen and to follow simple directions given by the teacher. As the teacher sings and demonstrates each song, the children should be encouraged to respond rhythmically. Taking time to say the words without singing helps to clarify the concepts and gives the child a chance to verbalize. The first songs should be simple, expressing a single idea or thought. Careful choice of a song that ties in with the other activities in the program helps to provide continuity, increasing the probability that the shy child will begin to verbalize more freely.

Selection of songs. A great deal of effort has gone into the choice of songs that would be appropriate for the purposes of the Early Training Project. This means that first of all, we chose songs that were highly attractive to the children, usually songs that involved action and a clear rhythm. We also attempted to select songs that would relate to the child's background of experiences. Within these limits, we chose songs in terms of their musical value; we wanted the songs the children learned to have artistic merit, as well as to promote the variables with which we were concerned.

Certain songs were selected to promote concept development. We were able to find many songs or singing games that involved counting. "Ten Little Indians" is an example of this; "This Old Man, He Played One, He Played Knick-Knack on My Thumb" is another. The second song also teaches the names of body parts to the child who is not familiar with them. There are songs involving colors, such as "What Will You Wear, Jenny Jenkins?" in which the children may stand up when the name of the color which they are wearing is called in the song. Songs such as "Who's That Knocking at My Door?" were used to encourage the children to use the names, both first and last, of the children in the group.

Another category includes action songs. In this case we selected songs that were related to the experiences the children were having during the preschool. As an example of this, since the children all came to school on the bus, we used the "Bus Song." The children were already familiar with the background, so now they could learn specific action words.

> The wheels of the bus go 'round and 'round
> 'Round and 'round, 'round and 'round
> All through the town.
> The driver on the bus says, "Move on back" (repeat),
> The children on the bus go up and down (repeat),
> The horn on the bus says, "Toot, toot, toot" (repeat).

As the children sang they demonstrated such words as " 'round and 'round," "up and down," "move on back," and "toot, toot, toot." In this way the children, through their rhythmic actions in the songs, learned concepts such as over, under, big, loud, soft, in, out, high, low, run, walk, slow, fast, and many others.

Several songs were selected for the purpose of illustrating experiences that were familiar to the neighborhood in which the children lived. Considerable effort was made to include songs which fitted experiences that the children were having at a particular time. For example, this song about policemen was learned on the day that one child's father, who had recently been appointed to the police force, visited the class wearing his uniform.

> When the light turns red, we will stop, stop, stop.
> The policeman holds up his hand.
> When the light turns green, we will go, go, go.
> The policeman says, "Come ahead."

The song teaches color concepts as well as an understanding of signals and traffic lights.

Nursery rhymes. Nursery rhymes are valuable in developing a bridge between the singing activity and the purely spoken word; in addition, they offer possibilities for dramatic play. As the group sings the rhyme certain children can do the action. This requires that "actors" attend carefully to the words so that they will provide the proper action on cue. Some children will require extra help to encourage them to be one of the performing members. The teacher can make special efforts to have these children sit next to her and to follow her lead. This adds to their feeling of security and provides a model for the action, thus decreasing the probability of making a crucial performing and social error. Reinforcement in terms of social approval, as well as concrete rewards, hastens the children's willingness to engage in such activity. As they learn the songs and master the dramatic play, spontaneous choice of "the one to do next" will reflect the sense of achievement and self-assurance that they have gained. Some of the nursery rhymes that fall into this category and have possibilities for dramatic interpretation are "Jack and Jill," "Little Jack Horner," "Sing a Song of Sixpence," "Humpty-Dumpty," "Little Bo-Peep," "Little Miss Muffet."

Singing was excellent for stimulating verbal activity in some of the children who seemed very unwilling to speak in even a one-to-one relationship. Some who tended to respond with monosyllables or with smiles and ducking of the head would often begin to sing somewhat quietly with the group, where they could not be observed, which at least gave them some opportunity to practice oral language.

Our general approach to teaching songs was the usual one for preschool groups in which someone, ordinarily the teacher or one of the aides, presented the song, usually with piano accompaniment, and gradually invited the children to join in stanza by stanza. The main difference we made in working with songs was to allow for considerably more repetition than might be ordinarily expected. We found that this was not only necessary, but also very much enjoyed by the children. To promote language development in individual children, the songs that we used in the large group were also used in the small groups, where four or five children could sing together and review the songs they had learned in the large group.

As suggested in the section on attitudinal variables, one of the problems the culturally deprived child has is a lack of predictable environment. For this reason many aspects of our preschool situation were set up especially to make things predictable. Songs were included as one element of this, since songs do give a temporal spacing that is completely predictable. As the preschool drew to a close, some of the children were beginning to enjoy the unpredictable, but most still seemed to profit by a certain amount of repetition and routine.

We did not use many singing games during the first summer of the Early Training Project, but during the second and third summers we taught the children to enact some of the simpler singing games which demand understanding and following directions. Sometimes we worked in small groups, sometimes with two small groups together, and later as the total group. We included such songs as: "Looby Loo," "Go In and Out the Window," "Three Blind Mice," "The Farmer in the Dell," "Blue Bird," and "Shall I Show You How the Farmer." These songs involved listening closely to directions, and promptly responding at appropriate points in the song. We found such singing games particularly helpful in teaching the children to respond to the verbal content of a situation, rather than to pick up their cues from other, nonverbal, aspects of the situation.

Rhythmic activities. Children enjoy all kinds of music, but especially music which calls for rhythmic involvement. The worker with this age level devotes little time to the more passive aspects of musical enjoyment. With records, piano, or other instruments the children can learn to express the rhythm in a variety of ways, from keeping time with their hands (loud and soft), walking in time, marching, and skipping, to expressive arm and hand movements. Whatever the child feels he should be encouraged to express through his own rhythmic interpretation. Both the teachers and the children can express choices concerning the kinds of meaning they want the group to act out.

Rhythmic activities were especially useful to balance some of the more structured aspects of the program. The children appreciated the opportunity to express themselves freely by responding with bodily movements to the music; they marched, stamped, hopped, trotted like ponies, and flew like birds. In the beginning, we found that these youngsters were quite timid and presumably unimaginative in interpreting music, but with some encouragement and examples from the adults and other children, the majority of the children could free themselves to enjoy participating in the activities.

Rhythm instruments. We assembled the usual preschool band instruments, from drums and triangles to rhythm sticks. It is possible to make relatively fine auditory discriminations by learning to identify the various rhythm instruments through sounds alone. The appropriate use of rhythm instruments demands careful listening and following directions; it demands keeping time with the group; it also provides opportunity for learning such concepts as loud, soft, fast, slow, and together. Most of the children developed considerable facility with the musical instruments. Those who failed to attend and to come in on time with their instruments were likely to be scolded by the other children; in this way the children themselves became reinforcing agents in the attempt to teach each other to listen and to follow directions.

Listening to records and tapes. Along with the songs, we selected records with reference not only to their musical value but lso to their potential for stimulating language and concept development. We selected many songs chiefly for their musical value and or the sheer enjoyment that the children received from listening o them and joining in. Therefore, we had a sizable collection of he simple folksongs, cowboy songs, and Indian songs. We also sed a fair amount of some of the simpler classical music for rest ime.

We found that stories with musical scores were attractive to he children, and that they would listen to them over and over gain. Records that were especially appropriate for quiet time were A Walk in the Forest" and "Muffin in the Country."

There are also a certain number of activity records which ould be used the same way as the activity songs. Such records s "Let's Be a Fireman" and "Let's Play Zoo" were especially elpful for some of the teachers of small groups who did not have dequate singing voices.

We made a limited use of prerecorded tapes, and we might use nore if we were repeating the study, because such tapes allow a egree of flexibility not entirely possible with the records. We used hem for sound effects in connection with puppet plays, or for ecording sounds around the neighborhood and then asking children to identify them. They also served as excellent supports for on-musical teachers who could persuade some of the more musial to prerecord songs for them to use in their own small group ctivities. Obviously, prerecorded tapes were useful for special ongs not easily available, and also for original songs, when it was lesirable to present them through some other means than the eacher. Sometimes it was desirable for a woman teacher to have he song presented by a male voice, and vice versa. The children vere fascinated by tapes of their own singing; such taping was used lso as a way of furthering their language development, and for eneral building of the feeling of self-worth.

ARTS AND CRAFTS

The culturally disadvantaged child, coming from a very lepressed environment, has few opportunities to enjoy the beauty hat is an accepted aspect of life for the middle class child. His everyday clothes are probably hand-me-downs, in poor repair and drab colors. The interior of his home is often bleak and in a state of deterioration, reflecting the apathy or despair the family feel. On the other hand, his surroundings may go to the other extreme, emphasizing the garish, the cheap but flashy, lacking the kind of aesthetic coordination that one finds among the more affluent. The exterior of the building in which he lives is usually in disrepair, often in a state of crumbling decay which is oppressive. If he has a yard, more than likely it is filled with oddments and scrap collected for uses long forgotten, or, if his play area is the street and the sidewalks which border it, he sees the monotony of grey cement and black asphalt.

The supervision of the culturally disadvantaged child is often left to an older brother or sister who is charged with the responsibility of keeping the younger one out of trouble. His opportunity to explore his environment is therefore drastically curtailed and he has little chance to try new things, to encounter experiences that add excitement and drama to his existence. In a world where one has little that he can call his own, where everything must be shared, even the clothes that he wears from day to day, there is little or no opportunity to develop a notion of an individualized self who acts effectively upon his environment, producing and creating. What one gets, one must fight for; a possession out of sight is lost.

Art and craft activities allow the child to experience novel materials in a much less structured fashion than is possible in some of the other activities in the program. Here he can experiment with color, with design, with a variety of media in ways that produce a product that is uniquely his own. Once he has learned there is an obtainable goal, learning to set his own standards of work develops persistence and the motivation to achieve. The objective product of his labors affords the teaching staff an opportunity to reward his effort materially and socially. His work can be displayed where his peers can appreciate it; he can take it home, providing a contact between school and home built upon demonstrated proficiencies. Many of the media provide an opportunity for an emotional outlet that is lacking in much of the demanding environment of the preschool. He can thump and bump and pound the clay. He can get into the gooey finger paint and fashion all sorts of designs without the fear of reproof for getting dirty. He can discover that pounding a piece of wood causes less dfficulty than pounding a classmate.

Art and craft activities are particularly useful in developing the child's sense of texture and form, and in giving him a chance to explore tactually the objects in his environment. Development of sensory or tactile discrimination with art media is a particularly important objective. Art activities are excellent occasions for the child to express what he has experienced; for instance, after field trips the children should be given a chance to illustrate what they saw and what they did. In addition, the child can have the experience of illustrating stories that have been read to him or told to him, and so develop a contact with other activities that go on in the program. In these activities the emphasis is placed upon active participation, upon manipulating and constructing simple things with the hands and body leading to a valuable end product. Such experiences foster a relaxed and non-threatening atmosphere which facilitates verbal productivity. The involved child soon forgets the presence of adults and even of his peers and can freely express what he is thinking about. As he talks about his efforts, the teacher can help shape speech patterns in an informal and relaxed way. It should be noted that while there is more freedom in art and craft work, the teacher is still instructing; she is constantly on the alert to capitalize on the incidental verbalization, directing and demonstrating all the while. In addition, these activities provide still another way of observing and evaluating the progress of the child in his socialization to the school classroom. Such evaluations can help the teacher more effectively to plan subsequent activities which will help to further the child in his development.

The following materials and activities seem to be particularly relevant and useful in obtaining objectives of the Early Training Project.

Finger painting. Finger painting is an excellent first project in art for children from a deprived background. It gives them the opportunity to be free from the demands of tools, to use simply their hands and arms in developing their project. Usually the child will be timid about exploring this medium until he is reassured that getting his hands and arms dirty with the finger paint is all right. Although his initial attempts are usually not much more than a big smear, he will enjoy the activity greatly. Tempera paint mixed with liquid starch forms the basic material. It is a good idea to have finger paint paper because the hard surface of the paper does not allow the paint to soak in, therefore, much more manipulation is possible. Since this is a somewhat messy activity, tables should be covered with oilcloth. Having plenty of extra water and sponges to use to clean up is a good idea.

Children helping with these household chores are given another chance to take pride in their work and to gain a sense of responsibility concerning the physical appearance of their room. Helping with the housekeeping is a cooperative effort. The teacher can nurture the children's pride in their own classroom and can extend that pride to their own homes by developing skills which they can use to help care for the household.

Object painting. Many common household materials make excellent objects for painting with tempera. Toilet tissue rolls, paper towel rolls, and empty egg cartons are but a few of the possible objects which can be used in this activity. Learning to paint with one hand while holding the object with the other is a difficult task for the youngster. This activity gives the supervising teacher a chance to reward persistence and to develop the concept of completing one's work. A simple first project might be the use of egg cartons which have been cut up into shells. These shells are then painted and paper for head, feet and tail are pasted to the shell to make a turtle. The cardboard rolls can be made to represent barber poles or large peppermint sticks, and as the child paints around and around the concept of movement and of action can be developed.

Prints. It is not necessary to make an elaborate print block in order to have the satisfactions of this activity. Many objects in their regular form can provide interesting prints, and given the opportunity, the child can experiment with a wide variety of materials such as artgum erasers, rolled up pieces of cardboard, string, the ends of small cardboard boxes, or the corrugated end of a piece of cardboard to produce an aesthetically pleasing print. It is usually well to place the printing media in somewhat shallow containers so that the child can easily dip his printer into the paint. Paper plates are useful objects to be printed or painted upon. Eating mats for lunch time can be prepared by printing, giving an opportunity for everyone to see the child's work and to develop pride in what has been made. Wallpaper for the housekeeping corner can be produced in a similar way.

Easel Painting. This small group activity can best be facilitated with three easels which have painting surfaces on both sides. Each child should be allowed to choose colors from an assortment of bright tempera paints. If the dry tempera is used, adding starch to the paint helps to make it adhere to the surface of the paper as it dries. Help each child to be careful to prevent mixing up the paints in the containers; the mixed paints are prone to be rather dirty and brownish and most uninteresting. One way to cut down on the mixing is to have a separate brush for each color. You may mix and store the paint in large plastic bottles with tight covers and distribute it in relatively small amounts to the children in lidless milk cartons; this insures that plenty of fresh paint is available at each easel time. Large sheets of newsprint are the best kind of paper for this work; they can be taped to the easel with masking tape or clipped to the top of the backboard.

Painting at the easel is an opportunity for much conversation between the children, and this should be encouraged informally as the teacher asks the children to identify colors that they are using. She can stand ready to provide rewards for a well done bit of work. Initially, perhaps, the best criterion of a picture will be that the child has used persistence to finish his work.

Upon completion, each child's painting should be identified by his name, thus the child will begin to notice that there is a way of identifying his particular production through his name. Often children will want to paint things they have heard about in the stories that have been read to them. The teacher should capitalize upon this as she will then have the opportunity to ask the child to tell the story again or to explain the event depicted in his picture. While the keynote is the opportunity to express oneself relatively independently, the teacher should take advantage of the opportunities to work upon the variables important for the child's development.

Crayons and coloring books. Our experience with children from a deprived background has indicated that one of the outstanding deficiencies in their experience is extensive contact with many different things in a complex world. The simple line drawings in coloring books provide many of the needed contacts that the child could not experience in any other way. The opportunity to identify and to categorize people and animals in a variety of contexts is an important learning experience. His coloring response to these new things creates a kind of experience which allows him to broaden his conceptual world. Additional skills grow from the experience, such as hand–eye coordination, color concepts, and the opportunity for reinforcement in a bookish and school-related activity. In addition, coloring books provide a material reward that the child will work many hours to obtain. It is probably true that too heavy an emphasis on coloring books can dampen a child's creativity; on the other hand, when used appropriately, they can contribute to the motivational and conceptual development of children. If coloring books were the only experience with art media we would agree that deprivation is being fostered; the bad name they have acquired is probably because of such limited and limiting use. If they are selected for specific purposes, however, and as one of many experiences that the children in the training program have with artistic expression, they have a valuable place in the program of instruction.

Cutting and Pasting. This activity provides a unique chance for the development of finger and hand dexterity. The hand–eye coordination and small muscle control that is developed through this experience are important contributions to the child's development. He must learn to hold the paper with one hand and to cut with the other hand. The activity affords the chance to capitalize on safety procedures. One can develop the concepts of sharp and blunt. As his skills develop, the child will learn to cut out shapes and even to follow a designated line.

Cutting requires children's blunt scissors, newspaper, and/or construction paper. Using such things as cut up pieces of material, string, crayon, pieces of macaroni, and colored paper, the child can paste the pieces of material to another sheet of paper to make a collage. Learning to use paste without using too much of it, as well as finding effective ways to make materials adhere to each other, are accomplishments with an enjoyable end product. Many purposes are furthered by making chains from pieces of colored construction paper. In the beginning the child cuts out strips, then pastes them together in an interlocking fashion. The teacher supervising the activity has many opportunities to develop color concepts, the idea of first, last, and next, and to praise persistent activity. Counting the links in the chain reinforces the concept of a one-to-one relationship and builds number concepts.

Construction paper animals. Cutting out animals from construction paper so that the important body parts can be attached and made movable by means of paper fasteners can be useful in dramatizing the stories read to the children. A barnyard of animals can be developed in this way, leading to many opportunities for discussion and extension of the child's experiences.

Carpentry. Several blocks of wood, some large nails, hammers, and a small saw are good tools and materials to develop hand–eye coordination with use of the larger muscles and to provide the basis for safety considerations. Children enjoy learning to hold the nail and to hammer. At first you can expect fingers to be hammered as well as nails, and nails to be bent in the process of being hammered into the wood. Cardboard cartons can be used in construction, sawed and taped together with masking tape. The children can build barns and airplane hangars, as well as cupboards and tables for the housekeeping area. In the process, the child learns effective ways of handling his tools without endangering the well-being of others in the group. He may continue his work by painting and decorating what he has built after the construction has been finished.

Clay. We have used several materials falling under this general heading. The best seems to be water clay because it allows the child's production to harden in the sun and to be a relatively useful and permanent product of his endeavor. Flour, salt, and preservative mixed with water and food coloring can be used to introduce color at the initial stages of working with clay materials.

Enough of the chosen medium should be provided for each child so that his work does not become too little. He should be able to finish a sizable production, but if he begins his work with an inadequate amount of material, the end product will be small and less satisfying. In addition, it is important that the medium facilitate the development of hand muscles; for this, the large piece of material will be much more effective than a smaller one.

Learning is aided most by working in a small group with one of the assistants to supervise and help. The teacher or helper can demonstrate the use of the clay, be available for help with difficult parts of a child's work, and generally supervise the handling of the material. The child, however, should be encouraged to experiment, to pound and to toss the clay in order to discover its potentialities as well as to have the opportunity to release emotional tension. Working together, the children in the small group learn to share their efforts by helping each other and by talking about the work they are doing, as well as by sharing the objects and tools.

At the outset, the child who has not been exposed to such material will have a tendency to express himself in the only ways that are available to him. He will want to make balls and to throw the clay at other members of the group. He will be hesitant about sharing both the medium and the implements; he will probably want to make things with clay that he can wear, such as bracelets and ropes. This kind of behavior is to be expected, but, as the child is guided in the possibilities open to him with the clay, he will begin to develop more sophisticated goal-oriented activity. The teacher should be ready at all times to reinforce evidence of the child's efforts. At first he may produce simple rolled out strings or cords—the familiar snake—but as time goes by, the teacher should stop reinforcing such primitive efforts and look for more creative and ambitious products.

A finger-shaped bowl is a good first project. The child begins by flattening out his clay, placing it in his palm, and molding it to the cup-like shape his palm forms. Placing this product on a windowsill where the sun can dry it gives a quick and successful first experience. After the bowls have dried they may be painted with tempera, displayed for all to see, and later taken home.

LARGE MUSCLE ACTIVITIES

A proper balance between the more restricting sedentary activities and large muscle activities is essential for the young preschooler. The child between three-and-one-half and four-and-one-half years old has not yet gained sufficient muscle control to feel confident in his ability to engage in manipulating all types of wheel toys, in climbing jungle gyms, and in throwing and catching a ball. The culturally deprived child often has had no experience with equipment of this sort, so he may be especially inept at such play. On the other hand, he is probably much less retarded in the large muscle activity than in other areas, so that new activities involving large muscles will be more attractive to him than more sedentary occupations.

Large muscle activities seem to have an inherent attraction for most children, although the shy, immature child must be encouraged to participate. Because of the enthusiasm of most children, it is easy to allow this part of the program to become a free and independent activity with little attention being paid to the teaching and learning potential the activities offer.

The culturally deprived child soon learns in his home environment that he must scramble if he is to get his share, and that he must be prepared to fight if his rights, as he sees them, are violated. Large muscle activities afford the occasion for the child to channel his aggressions into more socially acceptable expression. This is doubly important for the children from a culturally deprived background when placed in the school environment where the social restrictions are far more confining. Learning to take turns, to share, to work together loading wagons, and to play cooperatively with a ball aid in the development of cooperative social skills necessary in group living.

Such experiences can be used to encourage verbal behavior and to teach the child to delay immediate gratification for a reward in the not too distant future. With a high adult–child ratio, it is possible to see that the child does not have the opportunity to ride a tricycle, pull a wagon, or whatever the desired activity is, unless he can ask for it. It is also possible to see that such verbal behavior is rewarded with the appropriate object as soon as possible. Taking turns, the time-honored preschool pattern, is an important element in learning to delay gratification. If a child must wait his turn and inhibit his impulse to take over by force, and then is rewarded for this restraint by obtaining his object, he is learning that deferring gratification in such circumstances is rewarded and also that it meets with social approval. The teacher should be generous in her praise of such deferring behavior, and should see that the other children are aware of the child who manages to delay successfully and also that they are aware that he does get his reward after the delay. Such learning is of course only possible in a predictable environment and one in which there is sufficient adult supervision that gratification can be confidently expected in the future.

Time should be set to discuss behavior standards. The children should help in the development of the standards and contribute the understanding of the "why" for each rule, as this gives them the chance to comprehend ends–means relationships. Dealing with abstractions and social concepts through language are necessary experiences for the culturally deprived child.

Tricycles, wagons, Irish Mails, wheelbarrows, and doll buggies are helpful in guiding large muscle activity. A large room or confined outdoor space should be reserved for their use. The confined area provides limits of operation and prescribes turns and sharing. The teacher can more effectively supervise and be involved in the learning process when the area has such limits. Striping the ground cover or floor with tape or paint for roadways and making traffic signs and stop lights, provide occasions for meaningful role play and safety instruction. Parking spaces, marked off with blocks into which the child must maneuver his vehicle, provide a challenge and a sense of accomplishment once the child has mastered the skill. Parades can be organized and made festive by decorating the toys with materials which have been developed in the art activities.

Each piece of equipment contributes in a special way to the development of motor skill. The hands steer and the feet are the means of locomotion for the tricycle; just the opposite relationship holds for the Irish Mail. The child who masters the Irish Mail has attained a high level of coordination and control. His aspirations and efforts to master the device should be encouraged and rewarded. Here competition with one's previous levels of attainment helps to set goals for future accomplishment and such motivation is rewarded and developed.

Wagons and wheelbarrows should be used to transport things as well as people. They can demonstrate their value as labor-saving devices by being used to carry wooden building blocks, articles from the housekeeping center, groceries from the store, and bag lunches to be eaten outdoors; these functions broaden the use of the wheel toys to other activities such as construction and dramatic play. Cooperation between hauler and builder is necessary and opens the occasion to reinforce learning from stories or visits by community helpers.

Punching bag. The inflatable plastic "Bobo the Clown" or an upright punching bag on a stand is an excellent tension releaser. Children sometimes come to school with pent-up hostilities because of the demands placed upon them at home. A younger child often becomes the brunt of teasing from older brothers and sisters. The problem is accentuated where the living quarters are small and the crowding is great. It helps in reducing such tension to have an outlet that does not endanger oneself or others and upon which the child can vent his bottled-up wrath.

Jungle gym. Heights and climbing can be fearful to many children, therefore the feeling of overcoming one's fears and "getting to the top" helps to develop one's sense of self-esteem and of control over his environment. As the timid child goes higher from day to day the teacher can reward his daring and accomplishment. As he becomes less fearful he can learn new "tricks," as swinging from hand to hand and hanging by his legs. The teacher, always present, can help him to conquer his fears by being ready to encourage his efforts and to catch him if he falls. The child's identification with an important adult role model is fostered through such help and assistance.

Ball and basket. Throwing large balls into a basket from ever-increasing distances fosters the child's hand–eye coordination and can be a vehicle for encouraging his achievement motivation. By carefully providing successful experiences while continually challenging his skill, the teacher will help to provide an atmosphere in which the child can compete with himself. At first he should stand near the basket and then gradually move away as he judges he can.

Relay racing. Children enjoy racing with the ball to a goal and throwing it back to another team member to continue the relay. It requires accurate throwing or rolling skills and running coordination. Group competition and cooperation are fostered. Children are enthusiastic about running races and it provides for the release of physical tension, as well as allowing the child to judge his own performance against that of others.

Swimming. For many culturally deprived children who have few opportunities to go to a beach or swimming pool, swimming is a new and exciting experience. If a public pool is available, as it was in the Early Training Project, it should be used to develop a swimming program. As well as actually learning to swim, learning the rules of the pool behavior, and enjoying interpersonal cooperation through the buddy system, are important results of this activity. Eliminating a fear of water in the timid children can begin by using a couple of plastic pools if no public facility is available. Water activities with hose and sprinkler should be encouraged just for sheer enjoyment of the activity.

Small locomotor toys. Trucks, trains, cars, and boats are excellent objects for dramatic play. Manipulating these toys, the children engage in much verbal give and take. The teacher can broaden their concepts of function and utility and can extend their knowledge by taking them for walks to watch a construction project in progress.

Rocking boat. The immature child who is timid about engaging in physical action will often respond well to this piece of equipment. It requires the active participation of several children and the shy child has an opportunity to be a part of the group until he gains enough self-assurance for independent behavior.

Rice table. In the Early Training Project we found an indoor sand box filled with rice to be an excellent substitute for the usual sandbox. It was easier to maintain, was readily available no matter what the weather, and offered some possibilities which sand could not offer.

The children made mountains, dug trenches, and loaded and unloaded their vehicles in much the same way one sees the sand pile being used. Large and small cans attractively painted serve as measures for estimating volume and for color discrimination. "Which can holds the most?" "How can we find out?" "Does it take two green cansful to fill the red can?" "Yes, the red can holds *twice* as much as the green can." Experimentation of this sort is valuable in developing concepts of volume and with the help of a kitchen scale can be extended to concepts of weight.

The experience of texture with the rice is enjoyable and can be extended to comparisons with other materials. Rice also makes the housekeeping easier than sand would, and the children are able to accomplish their task more effectively.

READING AND TELLING STORIES

The art of reading and telling stories takes on special meaning and importance when working with disadvantaged youngsters. Many observers have commented upon the meagerness of the dramatic play of such youngsters; they seem not to have built up the richness of imagination that allows a child to remove himself in fantasy from his everyday life, often bleak indeed for the deprived child, into the world of *Alice in Wonderland* or *The Little Mermaid*. Even more, such children do not receive the encouragement they need to develop an interest in books or to gain the necessary skills for handling them properly. Their parents at best are probably poor readers attaching little importance to reading; they may, in fact, be genuinely suspicious of the written word. Furthermore, few reading materials are available at home, even if the children did desire books. The culturally disadvantaged child needs someone who understands his life and the circumstances from which he comes to help him develop an interest in books and the world of make-believe. His teacher is the bridge providing the fundamental orientation to books and book-related activity that the culturally deprived child so sorely needs.

A key issue in programs of preschool training for culturally disadvantaged children is that of the ratio of adults to children. It is vital that the ratio be high, preferably one to five (or six) with the three and four year olds. This is necessary so that the teacher can be sensitive to the individual differences among the children with whom she will be working. She must be able to assess each child's abilities, his motivations, his attention span, and his interests in order to maximize the effectiveness of the program for each child. Stories provide one of the best opportunities for her to interact with the child and to assess his status. Since this assessment is an ongoing process, it can only be done effectively if the adult-child ratio is high.

The teacher's initial assessment of the group's experiences provides a basis for her selection of stories that will be intrinsically interesting to the children. She begins with material within the grasp of the child: make-believe stories of animals which have plot, repetition of word patterns, and opportunities for the child's participation in such things as making animal noises or some other key repetitive theme, are a good point of departure. At first, the stories should be told with the book in hand. The teacher is then free to use all of her talents in dramatizing the story. After several tellings, the book is introduced with its colorful pictures which depict the sequence of events. The handling of the book is very important at this point because the children need to be able to see the pictures clearly. A little practice in reading the story upside down can help the teacher in this phase. As the children gain skill in attending, the teacher will be able to hold the book up and read from the side; with familiar stories, a child can be chosen to hold the book so everyone can see and to turn the pages on cue.

Telling and reading stories should never be a passive experience. As the children gain familiarity with stories that are read again and again, ask them to anticipate the event, "What's going to happen now?"; to supply the next part of the story, "And then what did he say?"; to tell what is happening in a key picture; or to describe how one of the characters must feel at a certain point in the story. Such analysis has much to commend it to the program for the child: through his interest he is being asked to verbalize, to use language effectively and colorfully; he is being encouraged to attend to the sequence of events and to put his sensory experience to use. Most importantly, as the child responds, the teacher is in a position to reinforce those responses which are essential to the child's development.

As the child's skills develop he should be allowed to tell stories that are familiar to the group. In this way, he learns to manipulate the book, to use pictures as cues for the sequence of events in the story, and to develop time concepts in his telling. The small group may want to act out parts in some of the stories that lend themselves to dramatic play. The group can use their art period to make simple costumes and perhaps "do" the story for other members of the class. The story also gives the chance for the children to illustrate the action themselves. Making a picture book about the story with their own illustrations gives them the opportunity to develop pride in their own efforts and also furnishes a reward for their work.

Stories provide the central theme as well as extensions of the study units in the program; therefore, a wide variety of reading materials should be available to the group. An interesting library corner where the child can go and select a picture book to look at after he has begun to develop an interest in books is essential to the program. The books should be selected to cover a wide range in content as well as levels of difficulty. Some of the books should be merely picture books depicting such things as community helpers, animals, trucks, ships, airplanes, birds, fish, or other things common to the environment. Illustrated story books of the children's classics, such as *Goldilocks and the Three Bears, The Three Little Pigs, Peter Rabbit,* and the like, provide a transition step from the skills of picture identification to the introduction of a simple plot and sequence. The last step is a giant one, through which opportunities available to extend the child's concepts are greatly increased.

Filmstrips, records, and movie films are available for many of the classic stories, and such audio-visual aids extend the effective range and use of the story. The listening emphasis inherent in the record, the opportunities to have the children tell the story from filmstrips, and the dramatic interpretation offered in the film are but a few of the values these aids provide.

The characteristics of the preschool children with whom a teacher is working may have implications for story telling and reading; for example, in the Early Training Project, the selection of books was influenced by the fact that we worked with young, culturally disadvantaged, Negro children who lived in a small southern town. Clearly many books, the traditional primary grade readers, that depict the White, Anglo-Saxon, Protestant world, with middle class, suburban homes, were inappropriate. The Early Training Project children certainly could not identify with racial-ethnic references, the socioeconomic level, the geographical residence, the life situation, or many of the interests and activities suggested in the books. Therefore, we attempted to use books with which they could identify, those which would not alienate them or serve to undermine their self-concept and self-esteem.

Initially we often used books that featured animal characters. In introducing our children to books and stories, special consideration had to be given to their short attention spans and their interests. Criteria for selection were brevity and interesting content. We selected those stories with action, humor, and/or repetitive aspects; the books were illustrated colorfully with clarity and simplicity. After they were successful in manipulating large books we provided the children with multiple sets of relatively inexpensive little books for use with the small groups.

A bibliography edited by Augusta Baker entitled, *Books about Negro Life for Children* suggested some of our reading materials. One book, for example, *Tobe,* was especially good in providing a figure with whom our children could identify. Physical features, living conditions, and the activities in which the characters were engaged made this picture story book particularly appropriate.

Books should be used as rewards to be taken home and enjoyed as personal possessions. In the Early Training Project we found that the children would work for extended periods of time for such rewards after a period of exposure in which they learned the value of books. Taking home a familiar book to "read" to their parents and their younger brothers and sisters extended the bridge into the home, creating an intrafamily or vertical diffusion of the effects of the program. Too often we have tried to motivate parents to help their children by preaching to them about the things that they should be doing, hoping to change parents so that a change can be extended downward to the child. However, we have often found that by working effectively with the child, his newly found interests and needs can diffuse upward to the parents as well as to his brothers and sisters, thus setting in motion a stimulating cycle from which both the parents and the child may benefit.

At home the child continues to develop the mechanics of handling a book as well as the attitude that books are sources of pleasure. A book also can become an important personal belonging for the child as a cultural effect or school-type material that is sometimes missing in the disadvantaged homes. In some of the homes, personal possession of any item or object is often not the rule, but rather the exception to group use of whatever is available whenever it is required. In this situation, something to call his own can help the child develop a sense of pride in ownership, as well as a sense of responsibility for the care of his belongings.

The presence of books in the home offers the potential for adult–child interaction that is verbal, rather than nonverbal, in nature. Reading to the child may be an interesting opportunity for a parent, or an older sibling or relative, to have contact that is activity-centered. We found that adults in the home may be "taught" ways of reading stories to their children. Parental participation was also elicited through the use of the children's classics that the one generation could share with the other. Through the encouragement a parent gave a child in the use of books at home, or the actual involvement of the parent and child in reading activities, the parent became the rewarding agent.

Finally, books in the home as sources of information and entertainment have some advantages in contrast to television viewing. The child's attempts at verbalization and the rewards he receives for his efforts are two important factors in language development. This helps to explain why story reading and discussion prove effective where television fails the culturally deprived child. The fleeting "eye" of the television camera is not under the control of the viewer; the only repetitive content is in some commercials (and this is a partial explanation of why children can memorize them, and yet be unable to describe or interpret other things they have seen on television). In contrast, potentially, books can be brought under the control of the reader. The selection of content and the speed of presentation can be controlled simply by turning the pages. The child may delight in "bringing back" the content at will—by turning the pages to a particular sequence of pictures or by asking someone to "read the story again." Books provide greater opportunity for verbal interaction between parent and child than television does chiefly because of such control over the speed of presentation.

SPECIAL ACTIVITIES

Whether the culturally deprived child lives in a city, a town, or in a rural area, the geographical range of his experience is sharply circumscribed. His outside world includes only the immediate neighborhood, the corner grocery, sometimes the church or the home of a close relative who lives much the same as he does. While much can be learned within the confines of this restricted neighborhood, the adults peopling it have neither time nor ability consciously to see that the child benefits from his contacts with nature and the activities of his community.

We chose the experiences discussed in this section because of the rich opportunity each presents to expand the child's experience from home to the extended community. The activities capitalized on the natural environment, the day-to-day work in home and community, and stressed the interdependence of men as social beings. Time and events that are part of the common heritage of our culture form an integral part of the program.

We made an effort at all times, however, to plan special activities in keeping with the child's present capacities and ability to deal with his world. We were particularly careful about trips to places which were quite different from the child's home and school environment. New information is important for the children but it should not run ahead of their ability to process the information, that is, to integrate it into their present understanding of their world.

Housekeeping. The housekeeping or playhouse area of the classroom provided a scaled model of the home where dramatic playing can define family roles and encourage verbalization. We found the role of the father to be vague to the children, as one might expect in a matrifocal culture where the father is often absent from the family. Although the teacher can help to clarify concepts, it is important to have male role models working in the program with the children and to include in this activity items such as hats, neckties, newspapers, lawn mowers, and the like, for the boys to use in dramatic play. Extending the dramatic play to the wheel toys and blocks, with which a boy can be working, helps to round out the model and to make his male role more specific. Dramatic play can help the teacher in evaluating the conceptions and misconceptions of the children, so that she can plan to fill in gaps of knowledge with subsequent activities.

The equipment used in the housekeeping corner should be simple but clean and attractive. Kitchen equipment, cleaning gear, beds for dolls, throw rugs, cupboards for storage, and small clothes racks for dress-up clothes should be provided. The activity can be extended to picture study of furniture, food, clothes, and occupations. It is important to plan this area to be somewhat congruent with the child's own home furnishings—a clothesline and clothespins, for example, will be more meaningful to the children than an automatic dryer.

One important aspect of the activity is the opportunity to develop communication between adult and child. Deprived children usually show reticence in their relations with adult strangers; while communication with peers may be fairly free and easy, the child is apt to be passive with adults. As the teacher plays with the children, some of these barriers can be broken. Nevertheless the teacher stands as a model for clear speech; verbal behavior should be reinforced by the verbal approval of the teacher. While acting as a participant, a reinforcing adult, a role model, and observer, the teacher uses dramatic play as an essential learning method.

Grocery store. Most children will have had experience with neighborhood grocery stores. Following a trip to a supermarket, the development of a store in the classroom offers a wealth of experience related to the cognitive development of the child. It also helps to span the gulf between the training program and the home, providing continuity in the child's mind between school activities and home activities. As the containers come in to be added to the shelves of the grocery store, turns can be taken in identifying each product. Items can be classified and arranged on the shelves by types. Dairy products should be given a special place to preserve them. Cleaning products, toiletries, paper cutouts of fresh vegetables, and meats should all be included. As the children learn to identify and classify, all the containers can be swept from the shelves and scrambled willy-nilly into a pile that the group may rearrange by categories.

The teacher can bring items not usually found in the culturally deprived home, taking the opportunity to discuss the origin and use of the product. New foods should be sampled for taste, odor, its place in a meal, and the differences between the raw product and the prepared form. Many of the children in the Early Training Project had never seen or tasted a prune before. When a box of the dried, wrinkled, fruit was brought to school, some of the children were hesitant about touching it. The teacher opened a prune and the seed was examined; she presented pictures of the tree and the ripe fruit. The children asked how prunes are prepared and why they are good for you to eat. Then the teacher encouraged each child to taste the prunes. Their cheeks were ballooned for half a morning as they enjoyed a new and different product.

Dramatic play can be used to broaden the experience; pretending to be clerks, with cash registers, and token money given the children experience in counting, checking out items, and choosing products wisely from a health standpoint. Initially it would be well to have the price of each item simply one token. The child is allowed to have as many tokens as he can count: the higher he can count the more the reward he has in purchase power. Later the symbol can be added to the token—ten cents is worth ten purchases—which extends quantitative concepts beyond the one-to-one relationship. Tokens can represent pennies; nickels and dimes and simple change can be made.

Walks and rides. Many experiences that are available in the immediate environment of the school and neighborhood are often neglected in planning special projects. Sometimes it seems that we fall into the trap of thinking that the objects of learning and the methods and procedures that are best for insuring a rich learning experience must be complex, although the contrary is more often true with young children. The alert, observant teacher knows that a bug, a leaf, a seed, or a nest has almost limitless possibilities for a learning experience. A walk around the school yard or a ride in a bus around the neighborhood has great resources for the teacher working with the disadvantaged child.

One of the main purposes of the identification walks is to help the child to be more observant in his immediate environment. If the teacher takes the walk prior to taking the children she will be better prepared to point out important things as the group moves along. A safety walk is always a good beginning in order to set standards for subsequent excursions by introducing the meaning of street and traffic signs. Point out to the children different types of trucks, community helpers, or special building and weather conditions.

The science walk to identify birds, flowers, and other plant life is an interesting walk and can be repeated at each change of season. Seeds can be collected in the late summer and early fall for closer study under a magnifying glass. Identifying, arranging, and classifying these collections is a valuable follow through. Leaves and grass can be collected and used in the art activities.

After each walk the children can talk about what they saw. The teacher can feed extra material into the discussion in the form of pictures of specimens of related objects, thus broadening and strengthening concepts and rewarding the children's curiosity.

Science activities. Since the care of the culturally disadvantaged child is often left to an older brother or sister who is concerned only with keeping the younger one out of trouble and from being harmed, the child's curiosity is usually punished and discouraged. Whenever the child begins to evidence a rekindling of curiosity, it should be amply rewarded with recognition and approval. As children find that their curiosity is acceptable in the classroom they will begin to raise more and more questions about the "why" of things. Simple everyday phenomena noted in the questions that children ask can be directions for further experiment and exploring: "How does a bell ring?" "Why do some things float in water?" "Where does the light come from in a light bulb?" "What makes plants grow?" "How does a kite fly?" "What does a magnet pick up?" "Why does the snow melt?"

Children enjoy taking care of pets in the classroom; a bird, a pair of canaries, or a rabbit can be kept for a relatively long period of time to provide the opportunity to find out what different animals eat and how one cares for animals. Taking the responsibility for care and feeding helps to develop the concept of interdependence and the importance of following through with an activity.

An aquarium and a terrarium will add to the study of nature if care is taken in their preparation. Tropical fish are more interesting and offer broader occasions for study than the usual goldfish bowl. A toad and a turtle in a terrarium which has been carefully planned to be a self-sustaining, balanced living space, demonstrate the interdependence of animals and plant life. The function and use of various body parts of the animals can be studied.

Planting a garden is a natural sequence growing out of a study of seeds, through which the children learn that seeds are used for food and for other products that are useful to man. They can prepare the earth and decide upon what seeds to plant. Radishes grow quickly for a fast return on the children's efforts and can establish a time basis for evaluating the growth rate and progress of the other plantings. The children can keep a record as to the date of planting, the first plants to appear, first vegetables to be harvested, and the like, by pasting on pictures of the vegetables from the empty seed envelopes for headings of the time chart. Discussing the project and the needs of the plants for growth can be a continuing daily activity.

Comparing fresh vegetables with dried vegetables offers the children new and interesting sensory experiences. A small hot plate can be used to cook both types of vegetable so that each child can make a comparison of how they taste in the unprepared and prepared state. Health and diet considerations arise naturally from such exploratory projects.

Field trips. Field trips are an appropriate outgrowth of activities originated in the classroom, but they must be carefully planned and chosen for the maximum benefit to the program of learning for the culturally deprived preschooler. As part of the continuous efforts to expand the horizons of the child, there should be trips into the community to points of interest that have direct relevance to the everyday activities of the child, places which can further his social and personal development in some significant fashion. Field trips bear directly upon language and concept development as well as providing an opportunity for the child to come into contact with significant adults who may serve as role models or as examples of a particular community function. Becoming aware of the services that the community provides to further the welfare of its citizens is an important first lesson in the interdependence of man as a social animal.

Many trips will bear repeating because they will have so much to offer that is relevant to the variables toward which the program is directed or because repeated visits can help to encourage the habit of using a public facility. The library, for instance, falls in the latter category. After initial training with books in the classroom, and as the children begin to develop interest in books, a veritable treasure house is open to the child in the public library. Plans for the trip should include enough adult supervision to insure that each child has personal attention and help to make the experience enjoyable.

In preparation, the class should also discuss standards of library behavior and perhaps at least one kind of book to look for. Usually the public library will have a collection of children's books set aside in a special room, and perhaps even have a children's librarian. She will welcome the chance to tell a story and to present several books for the appropriate age level or some which are related to a particular classroom project.

A trip to a farm is an event that can result in many significant memories. The first-hand experience of seeing and touching a cow with her calf is unforgettable, and if the farmer has a vegetable garden as well, the children will enjoy seeing a variety of fruits and vegetables. Many of the activities on the farm can be discussed; a climb on the tractor is the crowning event for the boys. Perhaps a picnic can be planned with this visit, for what better way of reinforcing the knowledge gained about food production than to eat the product at the source?

The experiences enjoyed on the field trip should be allowed expression in the classroom through discussion, musical activities, art projects, and telling stories. Here the teacher has the opportunity to consolidate that which has been learned and to reinforce the verbal expression of concepts that the child has gained. A trip to the fire station is a fine opportunity to do some construction of a fire house for the small car play. Songs about community helpers always provide the chance for making the sounds of the bells and the sirens that children love. A lesson on fire prevention and the conditions which nurture fires will perhaps make the children conscious of the fire hazards so often found in their neighborhoods and the part they can play in preventing fires.

The following list includes trips which we in the Early Training Project found of particular value: farm, army base, pet shop, water plant, shoe repair shop, supermarket, furniture store, library, fire station, bakery, department store, hardware store, milk and ice cream plant, gas station, and museum.

Seasonal activities. Holidays and special seasonal events provide excellent opportunities for creative activities that allow each child to participate in the observance of such events and to identify with the customs and traditions that are part of the common heritage. He can see that he is a part of a larger social group having rich experiences to share with each other.

Halloween has real appeal for the young child with its costumes, scary stories, and the infectious fun associated with its observance. The child is rare who is not moved to talk and to express his excitement about trick-or-treats, witches, and clowns. Special songs are in order and are eagerly learned; also art activities, from making jack-o-lanterns to painting pictures of witches.

The emphasis for Thanksgiving is placed upon present day living and the many things for which children can feel glad. The teacher can use this opportunity to talk about farming and the gathering of crops before winter and about the many people who help to make our lives better, such as the grocer, the dairyman, the farmer, and other community helpers. This is the time to construct a "Thankful Turkey." The children can pick out pictures of things for which they can be happy and thankful and each places his own around a large turkey built of construction paper. This gives each child a chance to remember the things for which he can be thankful in his own way and within his own understanding.

In a similar fashion it is possible to use the other familiar holidays of the year—Christmas (and Hanukkah), Valentine's Day, Lincoln's birthday, Washington's birthday, and Easter and Passover seasons. Each of these gives opportunity for art activities and many new songs, as well as providing a basis of knowledge to bring to such holiday activities once the elementary grades are begun.

V

SCHEDULE AND LESSON PLANS

In this chapter we will discuss briefly the responsibilities of the various staff members and the procedures we employed in planning the curriculum for the project. It will be noted that almost every activity was utilized in some form or another to contribute to the overall goals of the project. We have included in our presentation a daily schedule, a layout of the physical plant, a weekly lesson plan, and several daily lesson plans with evaluation sheets prepared by the small group teachers.

The careful planning that went into the day-to-day activities was seen as one of the strong points of the program. The teachers were asked to evaluate every proposed activity in terms of its potential contribution to the major variables selected for emphasis in the project.

The head teachers were responsible for selecting the themes for each week, usually rather broad topics which would readily lend themselves to special emphasis of the variables. Among the topics selected were the following: *Pets and Other Animals, The Farm, Foods, Workers Who Help Us, Transportation, A Look at Our School, A Look at Our City, Seasons and Holidays, Homes, Machines and Tools, How Things Are Bought* (measurements and money), and *Elementary Science*. The head teachers would prepare outlines suggesting activities, films and film strips, books, songs, concepts to be developed, specific learnings anticipated, and review activities.

Program planning sessions for the staff were held daily from 1:00 to 2:30 P.M. For the first few minutes we discussed any special problems that had presented themselves during the day as well as any particular successes that we had experienced. We reviewed the day's activities, estimating their effectiveness and possible future use and suggesting changes. The small group teachers in particular found these moments most helpful as they were permitted to exchange ideas and profit from each other's experiences. The head teacher would then discuss the theme for the following day, telling of her planned activities for the total group meetings, and suggesting the kind of activities that might be appropriate for the small groups for follow-up exercises. The small group teachers would then discuss possible adaptations appropriate to their individual groups or to individual children.

The latter part of the planning session was utilized by the small group teachers for drawing up detailed lesson plans for the following day. In addition to plans for specific periods, alternate or buffer activity plans also were made to use if any activities proved ineffective. These lesson plans were checked by the head teachers the following morning for final approval. Following the completion of the planned activity, the small group teachers made an evaluation of the activity, as well as of the performance of individual children, and recorded it on the lesson plan. This served several purposes; it provided a record for future use; it served as an added stimulus for the teachers to improve and individualize their instruction; and it furnished the head teacher with information to follow the progress of the various groups and children. This made it possible for the head teacher to supervise the activities closely at all times.

SKELETON OUTLINE OF THE DAILY SCHEDULE

9:00	A.M.	Arrive
9:00— 9:45	A.M.	Group activity
9:30— 9:45	A.M.	Juice and crackers
9:45—11:45	A.M.	Small group activities
11:45—12:30	P.M.	Wash-up, lunch
12:30—12:50	P.M.	Small group activities
12:50— 1:00	P.M.	Group activity
		Review
		Prepare for dismissal
1:00	P.M.	Dismissal

The children reported for school at 9:00 A.M. They first met in the large group (twenty) in the homeroom with the head teacher in charge and the small group teachers assisting. In the beginning these periods were scheduled for approximately thirty minutes, but as the children gained in maturity and increased their attention span, the periods were gradually lengthened so that by the end of the last summer most of the large group sessions lasted approximately one hour. In these sessions the head teacher introduced and explained the topic chosen for major emphasis that day, and presented the materials and activities appropriate for children with a wide range of abilities and development, leaving the activities demanding a more individualized approach for the small group sessions. Extensive use was made of audiovisual materials such as films, filmstrips, prerecorded tapes, pictures, posters, and flannel boards. The activities were varied frequently, with regard to content and to the required response in order to maintain the children's interest.

Following the large group activities in the morning, the children met in smaller groups of five or six under the direction of the small group teachers who monitored the juice break and the noon luncheon. While the children were under the direction of the small group teachers, the head teacher was free to supervise the small group teachers and to work with individual children as the situation required.

Both the juice break and the noon meal were utilized as periods for learning activities emphasizing language development and concept formation. One example is the teaching of number concepts—"How many cups do we need today? Why do we have twelve cookies if we have six children? Why did we have ten cookies yesterday?" Also, introducing a variety of juices, fruits, and vegetables afforded the opportunity for learning new names, categorizing and classifying foods, and discovering their possible original sources. Questions about seeds found in apples and watermelons lead to interesting discussions: "What will happen if I plant these seeds? What kind of plants will I get? How are they alike? How are they different? Which one will bear fruit first? Which one will bear fruit for a longer period of time?"

The children met once more in the large group for a short

period of time prior to dismissal at 1:00 P.M. At that time the head teacher briefly reviewed some of the day's experiences and distributed materials that the children were to take home to show their parents.

The remaining time, approximately two hours, was spent in the more formally planned activities which were structured in such a way that the children were exposed to changes in activity and location as their level of maturity and attention span dictated. As would be expected, the more mature children could remain in a single location and engage in specific activities for extended periods of time, while the more immature needed frequent changes. The close and continued contact of a well-qualified adult with a small group of children engaged in appropriate and carefully planned learning activities greatly facilitated the individualized application of the variables selected by the project for major emphasis.

We have included some specimen daily lesson plans in order to give the reader a sense of the specific activities that were carried on with the small groups of children following a particular weekly theme, *The Farm*. The plans were selected from a cross-section of the group in terms of the levels of development for which they were prepared; therefore, no sequence is implied.

The first five specimen lessons were planned to further language development; the second five stress concept development. Lessons eleven through fourteen emphasize the development of perceptual-motor skills while lesson fourteen, along with lesson fifteen, is also concerned with attitudinal development. The essential notion is that the daily plans reflect a variety of specific activities for small groups of children which can be planned around the weekly theme.

Specimen lesson plans 11, 12, 13, and 15 have no direct tie to the theme of *The Farm*. However, they are specifically concerned with fundamental skills and attitudes and are included to indicate how the instructional program of the Early Training Project was designed to effect change in these areas.

1 inch = 16 feet

staff room

Since our major work with the children was conducted during the summer, we were able to use the facilities of a well-appointed school building. For each group we used one space as a "home room"; here we had a piano and a circle of small chairs at one end of the room. This space was used primarily for meetings of the total group. The other end of the room was equipped with movable screens so that it was possible for a small group teacher to work with his or her children without the visual distraction of other groups. Separate rooms were also set up for activities that needed a good bit of space or were noisy. The floor plan to the right indicates the general arrangement.

Floor Plan of Room Arrangements

WEEKLY LESSON PLAN: JUNE—FOURTH WEEK

The Farm

The natural curiosity of the preschool child leads him to inquire about the sources of things most familiar to him. The farm is the source of many foods, and, as the home of many well-known animals, is a natural area of interest to the preschool child. The interest may grow to include different kinds of farms such as dairy, poultry, and truck farms.

CONCEPTS

1. Plants and animals are important to us.
2. Most of our food comes from the farm.
3. Plants need sunshine, water, and air to grow and produce food.
4. The farmer raises many different plants—vegetables and fruits.
5. Farm animals are raised for different purposes.
6. Farm animals make different sounds.
7. Farm animals and their babies have different names.

MATERIALS

Books

1. *Come to the Farm*
2. *Little Red Rooster Learns to Crow*
3. *Wake Up Farm*
4. *Animals of Farmer Jones*
5. *Animal Families*
6. *Picture Book of Animal Babies*
7. *Train A-Coming*
8. *Farm Animals and Friends*
9. *Three Little Pigs*

Films

1. *Summer on the Farm*
2. *Shep, the Farm Dog*
3. *The Red Hen*
4. *The Adventure of Bunny Rabbit*
5. *Frisky the Calf*

Filmstrip

1. *The Farm*

Mounted Pictures

1. Domestic animal pictures
2. The farm
3. Farm animals
4. Four seasons on the farm

Vegetables and Fruits

1. Collected on field trip to farm
2. Purchased as needed

Simple Farm Tools

1. Hoe, fork, rake, etc.

Puzzles and Toys

Felt Board Cut-outs

SUGGESTED ACTIVITIES

Discussions

1. A farm picture.
2. The farmer, his family, and his home.
3. How the farmer helps us.
4. What does the farmer grow on his farm?
5. The seeds a farmer might plant.
6. Farm animals—use, their food, sounds they make, where they live, etc.

Poems, Songs, and Singing Games

1. "Farmer in the Dell"
2. "Barnyard Song"
3. "The Old Woman and Her Pig"
4. "Moo-oo, Moo-oo, the Cow Wakes Up"

5. "The Cow"
6. "The Happy Sheep"
7. "The Pig's Tail"
8. "A Hunting We Will Go"
9. "Shall I Show You How the Farmer"

Reading

Field Trip to a Farm

Planting Seeds of Common Vegetables and Grains

Matching Pictures of Vegetables and Fruits

EVALUATION

Do children recognize common vegetables and associate them with
the farm?
Have they learned new and higher order classifications?
Are the children using the newly acquired vocabulary?
Are the children responding more to language of others, particu-
larly language relating to the farm?

SPECIMEN LESSON PLAN 1

Theme: The Farm
Time: 10:30 A.M.
Station: Room 3

Materials:

> seven copies of *Train A-Coming*
> pictures of farmer, children, pig, cow, horse, rooster, train, etc.

Activities

> First show the pictures of the various individuals and animals and have the children learn the names of any they do not know. Then read the story twice. The first time discuss the pictures in some detail and relate them to the previous activities. If time permits, then read the story without interruption to let the children hear the rhyming.

Objectives

> language development
> names of farm animals
> names of vegetables and dairy products
> number concepts—counting
> position words

Attitudes

> The children are showing a readiness to listen to an entire sory, and this is a simple one that seems to appeal to children.

Adaptations and Buffers

> If necessary, resort to *Little Brown Bear* which the children enjoy so much.

Evaluation

The discussion before the story took more time than planned. The children were interested and attentiveness was better than usual, but we were not able to read the story the second time. Plan to do this tomorrow.

Notes on Specific Children

Mary occasionally called 4 objects 3, but always got 3 objects right. Sammy is making progress, but makes an occasional error. Allen made it through a reading lesson without leaving his chair—a first for him.

SPECIMEN LESSON PLAN 2

Theme: The Farm
Time: 10:30—11:00 A.M.
Station: Room 6

Materials

rabbits made in previous period
six copies of *Peter Rabbit*

Objectives

language development
increased interest in stories
verbal expression
reinforcement for previous activity
continued study of the farm

Activities

Inform the children of the planned sequence of activities. First, read the story of Peter Rabbit carefully, listening to the sequence and the dialogue. Assign the children their respective parts for the dramatization, and read the story again, calling attention to each child as the dialogue is read. Then dramatize the story using the rabbits the children constructed previously, with Samuel serving as Mr. McGregor and using the hoe as his prop.

Evaluation

The children did quite well. James needed considerable prompting, and the other children were assigned turns helping him. They agreed that making rabbits is more fun if you can use them later.

SPECIMEN LESSON PLAN 3

Theme: The Farm
Time: 11:00 A.M.
Station: Room 6

Materials

storybook, *Three Billy Goats Gruff*
crepe paper costumes

Objectives

language development
achievement motivation
delay of gratification

Activities

Read the story to the children; ask them questions and see how well they can relate the events. Then dramatize the story using the costumes. Make a chart using stars for those participating as an achievement motivator. Tell the children that after five stars have been accumulated they will receive a copy of the book.

Attitudes

They loved dramatizing the story and eagerly participated in it. We performed this story three times with various children pursuing roles or holding the book while others performed.

Evaluation

> We will begin having more stories for dramatization as we build up a repertoire of familiar stories. Each child received a star and we clapped for individuals as their names were called.

SPECIMEN LESSON PLAN 4

Theme: The Farm
Time: 10:30 A.M.
Station: Room 6

Materials

> tape recorder

Objectives

> language development
> verbal expression
> group singing
> achievement motivation

Activities

> Help the children to tape record "Jet Black Pony"and "Five Little Ducks," the songs they have been practicing. Use other songs as desired. Between songs, center the discussion around animals and record this too. Allow the children to hear themselves both singing and talking.

Evaluation

> This proved to be a very interesting activity. All the children participated, and asked to use the recorder again tomorrow; each one wants to talk some more so he can hear himself again.

SPECIMEN LESSON PLAN 5

Theme: The Farm
Time: 11:15 A.M.
Station: Room 3

Materials

crayons
paper

Objectives

language development
improvement of motor coordination
color recognition

Activities

Ask the children to draw pictures of the characters and the castle in *Once Upon a Time.* Begin by drawing the castle and then proceed by drawing the princess, a frog, and her golden ball.

Evaluation

This was a particularly good activity because it stressed colors, language, and motor coordination.

Notes on Specific Children

Mary, Jane, and Robert were very pleased with their work, as was the teacher. Sally and John had difficulty in completing the task in the allotted time.

SPECIMEN LESSON PLAN 6

Theme: The Farm
Time: 10:45 A.M.
Station: Room 1

Materials

paper with outline of the pig
parts of the pig
paste, pipe cleaners
vegeta-dolls

Objectives

concept development
language development
fine muscle coordination

Activities

First construct the pigs by pasting the cut out parts over the outline. While doing this discuss such things as ham, pork shoulder steaks, pork chops, bacon, pigs' knuckles, etc., identifying them with the body locations. Discuss the vegeta-dolls and learn more about vegetables and how they are grown on the farm.

Vegeta-dolls are made by using common vegetables available in the kitchen such as potatoes, carrots, for body and legs and an apple for a head, putting them together with either wire or sticks. The creative teacher can use a good deal of imagination in preparing these to get away from the trite and obvious; in one group, for instance, we used a stalk of celery as a long face with hair on one of the dolls.

Evaluation

The activity was generally successful. Not all the different pork cuts were properly identified as to location, but now the children associate all of them with hogs. The children volunteered that pigs' tails should be curled and had fun doing it. Most of the work was done well, so we chose this as an activity that should be shown to Mrs. D. (head teacher— achievement motivation). John, who finished his pig first, helped Dale, who was having some difficulty.

SPECIMEN LESSON PLAN 7

Theme: The Farm
Time: 10:00—10:30 A.M.
Station: Room 5

Materials

    construction paper
    rabbit parts
    cotton balls
    paste
    black crayon

Objectives

    concept development
    proportions and the relation of head and body
    "brown" as a color concept
    characteristics of rabbits
    number concepts

Activities

The children make rabbits by pasting together the cut-out parts using cotton balls for the tails.

Evaluation

The children enjoyed the activity and were especially interested in the rabbit tails. They readily participated in the discussion of the number of ears, feet, and other body parts of the rabbit. There was also a discussion concerning the carrot which the rabbit held. Later, carrots were served at lunch and all of them were eaten.

SPECIMEN LESSON PLAN 8

Theme: The Farm
Time: 11:15 A.M.
Station: Room 4

Materials:

large hollow wood blocks of varying sizes and colors

Objectives

concept development
number concepts
color concepts
memory
language development
achievement motivation

Activities

Ask the children to build the tallest tower that they can. Assign each child two colors that he may use in constructing the tower. Ask them to answer the following questions: "Who built the tallest tower?" Who used the most blocks in his tower? Who used the least? Who used the most blocks of any one color?" Help them to remember the colors they used and the number of blocks in their tower to report tomorrow.

Evaluation

As on the previous occasion the children engaged in a great deal of verbal interchange.

Notes on Specific Children

Samuel and John were in real competition trying to build the tallest tower. John won because he quickly monopolized most of the large blocks; however, Samuel was proud of the fact that he used the most blocks in his tower. Mary acted as a self-appointed referee watching to see that no one used the wrong color, as Anne was inclined to do.

SPECIMEN LESSON PLAN 9

Theme: The Farm
Time: 9:45 A.M.
Station: Room 1

Materials

assorted pictures for classifying—animals, plants, furniture, clothing, etc.

Objectives

concept development—classification
language development—labeling
achievement motivation

Activities

Structure this activity in the form of a game. Place a stack of one hundred cards on the table: one child will draw a card; the next will name the object; and the third will categorize it. If no errors are made, put the card aside, otherwise return to the bottom of the stack. When all cards are disposed of, let the children go out for free play.

Evaluation

The children worked quickly and accurately in anticipation of going outside to play. They are ready for higher order classifications within categories.

Notes on Specific Children

Jim and Jack still have trouble with classification of clothing according to seasons. Kay needs to be rewarded for any indication to join in group participation.

SPECIMEN LESSON PLAN 10

Theme: The Farm
Time: 9:45 A.M.
Station: Room 3

Materials

crayons
scissors
paste
two mimeographed sheets, one with pictures of birds, animals, and insects (three each) to be cut out, and one divided into three sections with a picture of a bird, animal, and insect in each section respectively.

Objectives

concept development
categorization—animals, insects, birds
motor development—cutting, coloring
persistence—completing task with several steps
language development—learning names

Activities

Give the children two sheets of paper. Tell them to cut out the pictures from the first page and to paste them in the appropriate section on the second sheet, and then to color them.

Notes on Specific Children

Tom worked very rapidly and persistently, finishing early. At first Arlene would not join; she made several mistakes in categorizing either from a lack of knowledge or of concern; she refused to color the pictures and, with Sally, left the activity several times. Mike and Nancy worked persistently and carefully, not demanding as much encouragement as they had before. Sally had difficulty using scissors.

SPECIMEN LESSON PLAN 11

Theme: The Farm
Time: 9:30 A.M.
Station: Room 2

Materials

cardboard puzzles—made by pasting full page magazine pictures of human faces or other objects on cardboard and
cutting them into the desired number with a paper cutter.

Objectives

perceptual-motor skill development
visual discrimination
perceptual organization
language productivity
persistence toward goal

Activities

Give the children face puzzles and other paper puzzles to
assemble. Robert will work on puzzles of seven and eight
pieces. Jane—nine pieces and perhaps more. Carl six and
seven pieces. Mary and Sally—four and five pieces. Encourage the children to talk about their puzzles during and after
putting them together.

Evaluation

This activity was rather short, yet each child had a chance to
work two or three puzzles.

Notes on Specific Children

Jane solved a nine-piece puzzle and Robert did a seven-piece
one. Significantly Sally asked to do a seven-piece puzzle (a
picture of a dog) that she had been unsuccessful with previously. She had become disgusted with it when we were
doing puzzles last time, but now spontaneously asked if she
could try it again.

SPECIMEN LESSON PLAN 12

Theme: The Farm
Time: 10:00—10:30 A.M.
Station: Room 2

Materials

pegboard and pegs (100-hole—10 x 10 inches with ½-inch centers—and colored pegs)

Objectives

perceptual-motor skill development
motor discrimination
review of colors for James
counting exercise for James, Samuel, and Mary
achievement motivation (increase speed of performance)

Activities

Give the children various pegboard designs to copy from paper patterns. Robert and Jane will be given difficult ones using three or more colors; two-color patterns will be given to the other children.

Evaluation

This activity was fairly successful, though, when the group was given a difficult pattern to copy, they became rather easily discouraged.

Notes on Specific Children

Robert was given a pattern of four colors which utilized spacing or unfilled pegholes as an important part of the pattern. Although he had difficulty in doing this pattern (the spacing was wrong in some instances), the parts or different colors were in the correct relationship. Jane was given a pattern of one color utilizing spaces as an essential part of the pattern but she was not able to complete this by herself.

Both Jane and Robert will need more practice. James was fairly successful in copying a pattern of red and blue pegs alternating with each other and consisting of two oppositely alternating rows. Mary, after a little help, was able to copy a pattern of one color and two directions; the pattern consisted of only six pegs in one direction and a row (complete) in another. Samuel completed a pattern of one color in three directions, one of which was diagonal, although at first he was reluctant to attempt it.

SPECIMEN LESSON PLAN 13

Theme: The Farm
Time: 10:45 A.M.
Station: Room 2

Materials

one-inch colored cubes
beads of assorted colors and shapes

Objectives

perceptual-motor skill development
visual discrimination
number concepts
space relations
following directions
achievement motivation

Activities

Ed, Samuel, and Mary work with the block patterns. Ed is instructed to make a base of nine variously colored blocks in a 3 x 3-inch square, and then to place three additional blocks on top of the blocks along one end. Samuel and Mary are to copy his design. Then the three children are given verbal instructions to build a block house two blocks wide, six blocks on each floor, and three stories tall. After the three have agreed among themselves they are right, they may ask Mrs. D to come so they can relate to her what they were to do and have her check their work. Work with Jane and Alfred in copying bead patterns. Start with a five-bead pattern, and upon successful completion proceed to six, attempting to go as high as possible within the allotted time.

Notes on Specific Children

Ed, Samuel, and Mary worked in a most cooperative way and engaged in a great deal of verbal exchange. They successfully completed their task and were able to communicate it to Mrs. D. to her obvious satisfaction. She promised them story-books for their own tomorrow. Jane was able to progress to a twelve bead string, and Alfred to ten. This was one of the first times that he persisted at a required task for the entire period.

SPECIMEN LESSON PLAN 14

Theme: The Farm
Time: 9:45 A.M.
Station: Room 6

Materials

"Out of Doors" record

Objectives

perceptual-motor skill development
attitudinal development
auditory discriminations
following directions

Activities

Play the record through two times and ask the children to listen carefully. On the third playing ask the children to take partners and go through the motions mentioned on the record. Play the record again and teach them the words of the song, one line at a time.

Evaluation

The children had a great deal of difficulty following through on the directions. They seem anxious to learn and knowing the words to the song should help. More practice will be needed to make this a successful activity.

SPECIMEN LESSON PLAN 15

Theme: The Farm
Time: 11:15 A.M.
Station: Room 4

Materials

    wheel toys
    traffic signs
    traffic lights

Objectives

    attitudinal development
    visual discrimination
    color recognition
    sharing
    respect for the rules

Activities

We take turns on the wheel toys. Ask the "motorists" to respond to traffic signs and lights. General rules: Ask politely for a turn at the toys. Share after a polite request. No intentional bumping of "pedestrians" or "motorists". Disobeying of above rules will result in "suspended license."

Evaluation

The children were very cooperative in obeying instructions and rules and in recognizing traffic signs. They were much better at sharing than ever before.

Notes on Specific Children

Anne, Sally, and John correctly identified and responded to the signs. Marty still makes some errors but is improving. Mary identified only one sign correctly in six attempts.

VI

WORK WITH PARENTS

Our work with parents was planned to emphasize items that would be of immediate relevance for the children's attitudes and aptitudes concerning school achievement. We did not concern ourselves primarily with attempts to remedy the home situation in relation to family structure or economic problems; however, we did maintain an active contact with the social welfare agencies of the town, and, when it seemed appropriate, we directed individuals toward this service. On the other hand, we consciously tried to avoid running a program for parents that would have elements of social welfare within it. Although this is an important service, it was not part of the general program we delimited for our study.

GENERAL APPROACHES

The work with parents was primarily education-oriented, and was carried on by a former preschool teacher with training in sociology and social work. In her weekly contacts with parents, her work was directed chiefly toward three goals: (a) providing a bridge for the child between the summer school experiences of one year and the next (which involved familiarizing the parent with materials similar to those used during the summer with the child), (b) furnishing more information for the parent on the instrumental steps involved in school and occupational success, and (c) trying to promote in the parent greater feelings of her own worth and the worth of her child.

In about forty per cent of the homes there was no father present. Most of the mothers worked as domestics, maids in beauty parlors, cooks in restaurants, or in other somewhat menial jobs. Families were large, the median number of children being five, and in the majority of homes there were other adults present in addition to the parents—aunts, grandmothers, great-grand-mothers. The houses were lacking in the usual middle class con-veniences: hot running water was unusual and automatic washers were largely unknown. In addition, there were many health prob-lems, often resulting from inadequate medical care, poor nutrition, and general poor health conditions in the homes. The mothers with whom we worked, in large measure, carried heavy burdens which meant that both physical and emotional energy were apt to be sapped by living conditions. In our work with these parents the striking thing was that, despite the exigencies of their home life, the majority of them were able to rally the energy and to find the time to work with the children on the various tasks that the home visitor suggested.

Our major concern in working with the parents, other than that of providing a bridge for the child between his summer school experiences, centered around trying to help the parents develop a feeling of being able to cope, rather than the helplessness which seems all too often to characterize the extremely deprived indi-vidual. We tried to do this in several ways. One, for example, was giving the parents a picture of wider opportunities for Negroes than most of them seemed to have in the beginning of the study. Each month we provided a copy of *Ebony* for the mother, and the home visitor spent a short period of time going through the magazine with her, attempting to point out articles and pictures about successful accomplishments of Negroes, particularly those which were not related simply to entertainment and sports. Special birthdays of famous Negroes were also noted, as well as important news stories. Since ours was a research project, work was not slanted directly toward social action, but rather toward broaden-ing the horizons of the parents in order to foster a better under-standing of the role of the Negro American in today's world.

The home visitor also gave verbal recognition to the parent's concern for her child, and showed approval of the parent's efforts to provide for and work with the child on the various small projects. Often culturally deprived children have not developed a positive self-image because of the absence of adults who furnish approval and reinforcement. The same thing can be said for the parents. We found that such simple things as telling the parent, "You have a little boy to be proud of," was like water on parched earth.

Many of the efforts of the home visitor were aimed at showing the parent specific things that she could do with her child that would relate to future school success. We were not attempting to change the mother's whole personality organization, but rather to change her aspirations while providing her with a number of specific techniques she could use to help her child. An illustration of this is the home visitor's efforts to teach the parent how to read a story. At the start of the study, she found out that many of the parents were quite timid and backward about reading to their children, and hit upon the idea of role-playing with the parent. The home visitor played the role of the parent and the parent played the role of the child. This role-playing technique was subsequently used for teaching the parents several activities to enjoy with the child, working with the materials provided by the home visitor.

At the same time that she was teaching the parent specific techniques to use with the child, the home visitor was also setting weekly tasks for the child—often such seasonal activities as gathering a wide variety of colored autumn leaves—which demanded some participation by the mother in the task given for the child. Our hope was that this method could accomplish three things: (1) tangible results for which the home visitor could give recognition and approval on the next visit, (2) visible indication of accomplishment for the parent to appreciate, and (3) development in the parent of a habit of working with the child on the mutual accomplishment of the goal.

THE HOME VISITOR PROGRAM

By Della Horton

Participating in the home visitor program is a unique job which requires one to be alert at all times. To encourage parents to become interested, or more interested, in their children, you must be a good listener, playing the role of the doctor, nurse, minister, or other helpful friend. You must be able to explain technical language in plain words. In our program, for instance, each home visitor checks on the health of the child and encourages parents to take advantage of the free health services for the entire family which are provided by the local health clinic.

To go into a home and persuade the parent to listen to what you have to say, you must create an atmosphere of ease, transforming the apprehensiveness you feel when you first enter. Help the parent feel the need for interaction with the child and make your visit so interesting that you set the stage for future visits. One approach is to ask the simple question, "Mrs. Parent, have you ever been a teacher?" Of course, you know that the answer will be "No," but the two of you laugh together after you explain, "Oh, yes, you are; you are your child's first teacher and the only one he will have until he's ready for school." Because you have captured her attention, the parent is ready to listen and by this time may be agreeing with you. Now you explain how a child is or becomes what he is taught and exposed to in his preschool life.

With the parent's cooperation, we can expose her to many meaningful experiences that will enable her to help the child to grow. Ask more questions: "What does your child enjoy doing at home? What are his favorite games? Who are his best friends in the neighborhood? Does he invite the children in to play? Does he put away his clothes and toys when he is finished with them? Can he dress himself? What time does he usually go to bed? Does he take a nap during the day? Is he afraid of the dark? Does he have any fears?" Say to the mother: "You know, Mrs. Parent, children are different in their sizes, their abilities, and in almost everything. Each child must grow according to his own ability. By the way, how much time do you spend with your child every day? What do you talk about?" Usually the answer is, "Not much because I have to work and when I come home from work I have to prepare the meals." Show the parent you sympathize with her by agreeing that this is difficult, but be ready to suggest an activity that can be carried on while the meal is being prepared.

Speaking to the child, for example, she can say, "Tonight

we're going to have Irish potatoes; did you know there's another name for Irish potatoes?" The child asks what it is and the mother answers, "White potatoes." Then she may ask the child to feel the potato. "What does it feel like? Is it hard, like a rock? Or is it soft, soft like cotton? See the specks on it; they are called eyes. By the way, what do we do with our eyes? Can a potato see?"

Ask the mother whether she can see how much conversation and information can come from just one question about something she already has around the house. Let her know that enjoyable conversation should be encouraged at meal time for all the family, so that she may extend this activity into the evening meal. Give several similar examples, always using familiar things that you are sure are a part of the parent's experiences. As the child develops language ability, he will be able to express himself well enough to become curious about the things around him. Encourage him with further questions: "What vegetables do we see in our grocery store? Where do the vegetables come from? How does mother cook vegetables? Look through magazines; find and cut out all the vegetables you see. Next week you can tell me what they are." Follow up by suggesting an interesting story—"Watch My Garden Grow" or "My Vegetable Garden."

Another group of questions that could be asked while the mother is preparing the meal includes counting and making the child aware of various parts of his body. "How many hands do you have?" Two—a right hand and a left hand. How many feet do you have? How many eyes do you have? I'm cooking something for dinner that rhymes with eye. Can you think what it is? [pie]. Find something that we use in the house that rhymes with bread [spread]."

The mother is told always to praise the child for answers even though in the beginning she may even have to supply most of the answers herself. Explain to the parent that these activities provide recreation and relaxation as well as learning for both parent and child. You may be able to convince her that the home is the important center to develop life-long interest and skills and that parents must help to establish good patterns.

Show the parent how to read a story to the child by first reading it to the parent yourself and letting her play the role of the child. Ask questions about the story; be sure you are familiar with your material before you try to explain. Through our use of *Humpty-Dumpty* magazine, we develop a keen eye for likenesses, differences, and so on, and also provide many joint activities for mother and child. Such activities as home improvement, cleaning, fixing up, painting, drawing, coloring, pasting, collecting things, going for walks, and watching pet animals can be family affairs. All the activities suggested will make the child think and will help to develop his mind.

Dramatic activities are excellent for family enjoyment. I believe one of the most successful and effective activities I encountered grew out of reading the story, "Over in the Meadow." Each child was given the book, and parents were shown first how to read the story, which involves counting, following instructions, action, color, obedience, and many other concepts that require discussion. For instance, the following questions could be asked about the first verse: "What do you do when you *wink* or *blink*? Is there a difference between winking and blinking? What part of the body do you use to wink? What is sand? What do we use sand for? How does it feel? Where is the sun? When do we see it, night or day? Do we look *up* or *down* to see the sun? Now let's see if we can wink and blink."

For a subsequent verse we asked: "How many little toads were in the story? Who was talking to the little toad? By the way, can you wave your hand one time?" There were twelve verses in this story, and each one was treated in this manner. This required much interaction between parent and child as well as other members of the family. Every parent participated in this activity; some of them even drew illustrations of the characters named in the verses.

Another interesting activity was following the seasons. While looking for early spring flowers, you can search for the first leaves of the daffodils or buttercups. The child can measure their daily growth—using construction paper for the stem, he can add the amount of daily growth to his cut-and-paste plant until finally the full bloom is added. He can also look for green grass, buds on trees, or spring birds, the redbirds and robins. Ask him, "Where do the birds go for winter?"

Parents were encouraged to take the children to the post office, the library, or the supermarket and to talk with them about what they discovered there. We suggested that these activities be done as a family so that everyone could enjoy the feeling of sharing or togetherness—togetherness in action. Much discussion grew from consideration of the farm animals that give us our milk, meat, eggs, and also of pets on the farm. We even made the entire farm out of construction paper—the house, lawn, barn, silo, animals, mother, father, and so on. This was an excellent activity, especially because it showed some of the parents how much they could do to help their children.

Most of the parents were aware that all our activities were designed to make them feel needed and to try to prove to them that education is the key to the door of opportunity behind which lies the promise of greater economic independence and security for their children. We reaffirmed our efforts through constant use of the materials in *Ebony* and illustrations drawn from the wider social scene.

NEWSLETTER TO PARENTS

One small feature of our work with parents was a monthly newsletter that was circulated as an additional encouragement to the parents to participate in the program for their children. Since individuals living in deprived circumstances generally receive little personal mail, we felt such a monthly letter might have individual impact if it were planned appropriately. Thus, the newsletters were composed to be attractive, brief, and useful to the parents. They were generally reproduced on colored paper with a colored seal at the head of the letter which related to the seasons of the year— pumpkins in the fall, flowers in April, etc. We tried to make them attractive also to the children in the project, so that their interest might encourage the parent to make use of the newsletter.

We included emphases in each of the following areas:

1. Announcements about the project—generally referring to the monthly Saturday morning meeting held for the children during the school year.

2. Something to do to help prepare the child for school—

usually short, specific suggestions relating to things that parents could do with the child. They centered around seasonal activities and verbal interchange with the child.

3. Something to read to the child—generally simple accounts of events related to the children in the project. One month the "something to read" was about two new puppies that had been born to a neighborhood dog; another month it was about a trip one of the children had taken to visit relatives in a nearby city.

EARLY TRAINING PROJECT

DECEMBER NEWSLETTER

ANNOUNCEMENTS:

The second group (Mrs. Outlaw's children) will have their regular monthly meeting on Saturday, December 7, at the usual time. The first group (Mrs. Horton's children) will have their meeting this month on Saturday, December 14. In addition, all the children in both groups will have a Christmas party together at the school at 11:00 A.M. on December 14. Our bus driver will come by before 11:00 AM. that day to pick up the children in Mrs. Outlaw's group for the party.

SOMETHING TO DO TO HELP YOUR CHILD
WHEN HE OR SHE GOES TO SCHOOL

"Something to read to your child" this month has a suggestion for parents. Also, we have enclosed a postcard. Your child can take his or her crayon and color it to make a Christmas card to send someone, and then take it to the post office to mail. If your child would like to make one for his or her home visitor, Mrs. Horton's address is .... and Mrs. Outlaw's is
....

SOMETHING TO READ ALOUD TO YOUR CHILD
(A LETTER FROM MRS. HORTON)

Dear Boys and Girls,

Guess what? Martha Brown, one of the girls in the first training group, had a birthday last Wednesday, November 20th. She was five years old. The postman—or mailman, as we sometimes call him—brought Martha a large package. Martha wanted to know how the package had come all the way from another city to her home. She asked the postman what happens to letters and packages after they are mailed. Martha's mother decided to take her to visit the post office. Martha and her mother saw many things, letters being dropped in the letter slot, packages being processed for mailing; in fact, Martha took a tour through the post office. She enjoyed it so very much that she wants you to write your letters to Santa Claus, then ask your mother to take you to the post office to see how your letter is mailed. While there, if you ask the clerk to show you around, perhaps he will.

VII

BIBLIOGRAPHY

SOURCES OF EQUIPMENT AND MATERIALS

Sources of Equipment

Division of Surveys and Field Services, *Free and Inexpensive Learning Materials*. Nashville, Tennessee: George Peabody College for Teachers, 1964–1965.

> Grouped under 160 subject headings, this list offers over 4,000 aids for teachers, students, and parents. Each annotation includes basic information, such as the nature of the item, its size, and price, and the full name and address of the distributor.

Weber, Evelyn, and Lucy Martin (Eds.), *Equipment and Supplies: Tested and Approved for Preschool, School, and Home*. Washington, D.C.: Association for Childhood Education International, 1964.

> This bulletin was compiled by an ACEI committee; it includes a directory of manufacturers and distributors, their Canadian agents, and an index of items.

Recommended Bibliographies of Children's Books

Arbuthnot, May H., *Children's Books Too Good to Miss*. Cleveland: Western Reserve University Press, 1959.

Bibliography of Books for Children and Children's Books—for $1.25 or Less. Washington, D.C.: Association for Childhood Education International, 1964.

Eakin, Mary K., *Good Books for Children: A Selection of Outstanding Children's Books Published 1948–1961*. Chicago: University of Chicago Press, 1962.

Larrick, Nancy, *A Teacher's Guide to Children's Books.* Columbus, Ohio: C. E. Merrill Books, 1960.

West, Dorothy, and Rachel Shor (Eds.), *Children's Catalogue.* New York: The H. W. Wilson Co., 1961.

> This book is a catalogue of 3,310 selected titles with a list of particularly easy-to-read books for preschool children.

A survey of picture books in the juvenile collection or children's literature section of a public or school library can be a useful resource. Caldecott Medal Books and Newbery Medal Books are annual award picture books that may be used.

Sources of Records

Folkway Records: 121 West 47th Street, New York, New York 10036.
Rhythm Record Company: 9203 Nichols Road, Oklahoma City, Oklahoma.

> A large number of record catalogs are available from individual commercial recording companies. The two listed above are among the leading producers of records for children.

Schwann Long Playing Record Catalogue, W. Schwann, Inc.: 137 Newburg Street, Boston, Massachusetts.

> The catalogue, published monthly, is available from the publisher or in many local record shops and contains a complete listing of mono and stereo records; one section of the guide contains a listing of children's records.

Weber, Evelyn, and Martin, Lucy (Eds.), *Equipment and Supplies* (previously cited in section A).

> Two sections of this bulletin—audiovisual equipment and supplies and music equipment and supplies—give lists of children's records.

Sources of Films and Filmstrips

Educational Media Index. New York: McGraw-Hill Book Co., 1964.

> Compiled by the Educational Media Council and published with yearly supplements, this comprehensive index lists appropriate

films and filmstrips for preschool and primary age children, covering the levels from kindergarten through third grade.

Producers of films will send catalogues upon request. Some of the leading companies are Coronet Films, Encyclopedia Britannica, and McGraw-Hill Book Co.

University extension catalogues are another excellent general film rental source and are available from many centers. University extension centers of the University of Indiana and the University of Illinois are highly recommended.

SELECTED REFERENCES

Cultural Deprivation

Bloom, Benjamin S., Allison Davis, and Robert Hess, *Compensatory Education for Cultural Deprivation.* New York: Holt, Rinehart, and Winston, 1965.

Based on working papers contributed by participants in the June, 1964, Research Conference on Education and Cultural Deprivation at the University of Chicago, the book includes 134 references and 117 research summaries. These are classified under home environment and social class, language, cognition and learning, intelligence and aptitudes, personality and motivation, school achievement, and school programs and personnel.

"Education and Poverty," *Saturday Review,* XLVIII (May 15, 1965), 68–99.

The collection of articles in the education supplement includes the following: Vernon R. Alden on the Job Corps education and training programs and centers; Peter Schrag on "The Schools of Appalachia"; John Tebbel on the Abraham Kavadlo Springboards Reading Program for teaching deprived urban children; and Robert Coles, a research psychiatrist, reporting on a two-year study of transient farm workers in "What Migrant Farm Children Learn."

Passow, A. Harry (Ed.), *Education in Depressed Areas*. New York: Teachers College Press, 1963.

> Based on the July, 1962, Work Conference on Curriculum and Teaching in Depressed Urban Areas, the volume contains working papers prepared by eminent specialists on major theoretical and empirical considerations. Dimensions of study include the nature of schools, teachers and school programs, the psychological and social aspects of education, and the implications for educational planning.

Riessman, Frank, *The Culturally Deprived Child*. New York: Harper and Row, 1962.

> This book studies characteristics of the underprivileged—the economically and intellectually poor—as contrasted with those of typical American education and life. The author proposes program adaptations and teacher changes that will ameliorate some of the problems.

Education and Poverty

Conant, James, B., *Slums and Suburbs*. New York: McGraw-Hill 1961.

> Dr. Conant contrasts junior high school education in urban slum areas with its counterpart in affluent suburban areas. He gives observations and recommendations while considering such problems as school dropouts, curriculum, and organization.

Moore, Elenora, *Fives at School: Teaching in the Kindergarten*. New York: G. P. Putnam's Sons, 1959.

> The author characterizes "downtown fives" and "fives in suburbia," emphasizing many sociological and psychological influences that affect a child's education. The work is addressed to kindergarten teachers and parents.

Sexton, Patricia, *Education and Income*. New York: The Viking Press, 1961.

> This work is based on a study of a large, northern, urban public school system that provides evidence that the American public educational system is becoming less effective as an instrument of social mobility. The final chapter includes the author's comments and suggestions for changes with respect to finances, curriculum, further research, open records, and experimental programs.

Sociological and Psycholgical Aspects of Poverty

Agee, James and Walker Evans, *Let Us Now Praise Famous Men: Three Tenant Families*. Boston: Houghton Mifflin, 1941.

> Through pictures and prose the authors present a detailed description and depth analysis of white, cotton-tenant families in the late 1930's; the sensitive and perceptive treatment of the problem is notable today in relation to rural poverty.

Davis, Allison, *Social-Class Influences upon Learning*. Cambridge: Harvard University Press, 1948.

> This book is a classic work on the influence of sociological factors on education, a short yet comprehensive and authoritative summary of research conducted at the University of Chicago in the 1940's. The author's views have been cited in innumerable references since then.

Harrington, Michael, *The Other America: Poverty in the United States*. New York: Macmillan, 1962.

> This is an excellent, well-written, sociological account of the invisible, yet self-perpetuating, aspects of poverty which had an impact on the 1964 Economic Opportunity Act. The statistics and definitions are helpful as well as the author's understanding of many individuals and groups of "other Americans" who are disadvantaged.

Lewis, Oscar, *The Children of Sanchez*. New York: Random House, 1960.

A deep and intimate anthropological portrait of a Mexican slum family suggests generalizations about the culture of poverty throughout the world.

Silberman, Charles E., *Crisis in Black and White*. New York: Random House, 1964.

The present Negro crisis in America is analyzed with its historical roots and possible future solutions.

Sutton, Elizabeth, *The Migrant Child*. (Department of Health, Education, and Welfare, Office of Education) Washington, D.C.: Government Printing Office, 1963.

The author has been involved in research projects directed toward "knowing and teaching the migrant child." Many facets of life among migrant workers are reviewed and many specific instructional suggestions given.

Child Development and Intellectual Development

Mussen, Paul, and others, *Child Development and Personality,* 2nd ed., New York: Harper and Row, 1963.

The reference describes aspects of physical, intellectual, social, and emotional growth as interrelated phenomena, giving the reader a better understanding of continuity in the development of the child.

Stone, L. Joseph and Joseph Church, *Childhood and Adolescence*. New York: Random House, 1956.

This child study book is of interest to a vast reading public. It is an excellent "psychology of the growing person"—from prenatal development through the adolescent's journey into adulthood.

Wann, Kenneth, Miriam Dorn, and Elizabeth Liddle, *Fostering Intellectual Development in Young Children*. New York: Teachers College Press, 1962.

This book is the result of educational research that was directed towards understanding the needs of today's preschoolers and providing stronger emphasis on intellectual development in programs in early childhood education. The authors attempt to formulate their conclusions about the nature of intellectual development, the present experiences and needs of preschool children, and the implications that are discerned for curriculum and teaching methods.

Early Childhood Education

Hammond, Sarah, Ruth Dales, Dora Skipper, and R. L. Witherspoon, *Good Schools for Young Children*. New York: Macmillan, 1963.

This guide for work with three, four, and five-year-old children includes sections on schools for the young, curriculum-planning and teaching, and program organization in schools for young children. The authors highlight the need for understanding the child, his world, the forces influencing him, and the basic principles on which decisions are made regarding instruction and practice.

Hartley, Ruth, and L. K. Frank, *Understanding Children's Play*. New York: Columbia University Press, 1953.

The role of play and play materials is emphasized in this book, along with suggestions of ways that the teacher may encourage and implement play activities.

Heffernan, Helen, and Vivian Todd, *The Kindergarten Teacher*. Boston: D.C. Heath, 1960.

The authors include a description of the nature of kindergarten children and effective ways of working with them. Principles of child development lead to suggestions for personnel consideration, appropriate equipment, curriculum development, and fostering programs of cooperation between the home and the school.

Read, Katherine, *The Nursery School: A Human Relations Laboratory.* Philadelphia: W. B. Saunders, 1960.

This description of the Oregon State College preschool may be used as an excellent manual of procedures and teaching skills in the nursery school.

Rudolph, Marguerita, *Living and Learning in the Nursery School.* New York: Harper and Brothers, 1954.

The author gives insight into the nursery school child with an analysis of "the beginning of nursery school and its meaning to children." Her curriculum and evaluation sections are also interesting.

Sheehy, Emma, *The Fives and Sixes Go to School.* New York: Henry Holt, 1954.

Chapters explain how the child lives and learns through experiences in dramatic play, building, the arts, music, dance, and games. Other subjects also included are language arts, literature, reading, arithmetic, writing, science, and social studies.

Research Reports on the Early Training Project

Gray, Susan W., "Some Attempts to Change Attitudes in Culturally Deprived Children." Paper read at a meeting of the American Psychological Association, September 3, 1964.

————, "Some Implications of Research on Young Culturally Deprived Children." Paper read at a meeting of the American Psychological Association, September 6, 1964.

Gray, Susan W., and Rupert A. Klaus, *The Early Training Project: Interim Report.* Murfreesboro, Tennessee: Murfreesboro City Schools and George Peabody College for Teachers, 1963 (now out of print).

————, "An Experimental Preschool Program for Culturally Deprived Children," *Child Development,* XXXVI (December, 1965).

Klaus, Rupert A., and Susan W. Gray, "The Murfreesboro Preschool Program for Culturally Deprived Children," *Childhood Education,* XLII (October, 1965).